ANSWERS

August 1999

To my dear friend Lynn Bullock

I so much appreciate you

many kindnesses, and friendship

George Y Jarvis

ANSWERS

STRAIGHTFORWARD ANSWERS TO TOUGH GOSPEL QUESTIONS

JOSEPH FIELDING McCONKIE

Deseret Book Company
Salt Lake City, Utah

Library of Congress Cataloging-in-Publication Data
  McConkie, Joseph F.
    Answers : Straightforward answers to tough gospel questions /
  Joseph Fielding McConkie.
      p.   cm.
    ISBN 1-57345-355-2
    1. Church of Jesus Christ of Latter-day Saints—Apologetic works—
  Miscellanea.   2. Mormon Church—Apologetic works—Miscellanea.
  I. Title.
  BX8635.5.M39   1998
  230'.9332—dc21   97-41267
                                                                        CIP

Printed in the United States of America   72082-4620
10   9   8   7   6   5   4

CONTENTS

PREFACE

Some years ago in a military exercise I was taken with others of my unit deep into a rugged wilderness area in the dark of night. After having been deliberately disoriented, we were each given a compass and told to find our way back to an area designated as "safety." We were required to do so individually. We were warned of the various perils that stood between us and our objective, among them enemy patrols using dogs to find us.

By the coming of dawn, most of my unit was either in a POW compound or in the hospital getting patched up. Only a few of us found our way to "safety." Though my memory of that experience has dimmed, I am quite certain that one thought that did not occur to me that night was what a perfect parallel that experience was to our journey through life. True, life is more than a training exercise and its dangers are quite real, but the need to find our way through darkness and other perils to a place of safety is much the same. We all start our journey with the compass of a good conscience and the light of heaven from which we can take our bearing, and like that military exercise the consequence of each of our choices is very much our own.

As that military exercise involved finding the place of safety, so our journey through life involves making choices and finding answers that will either ensure our spiritual safety or, conversely, cause us to lose it. In that process we all must choose what we are going to believe and what we are not going to believe. No one in heaven or on earth can take that responsibility from us. Nor can anyone take from us the consequences of our choices.

The gift of agency was given to us at the time of our birth as spirits eons ago. "From the time of their spirit birth, the Father's pre-existent offspring were endowed with agency and subjected to the provisions of the laws ordained for their government" (McConkie, *Mormon Doctrine*, 590). That gift was renewed at the time of our birth into mortality (see Moses 4:3; D&C 93:30).

As the gift of agency is ours, so are its consequences. The two are inseparable. Teaching this principle, Lehi said: "Men are free according to the flesh; and all things are given them which are expedient unto man. And they are free to choose liberty and eternal life, through the great Mediator of all men, or to choose captivity and death, according to the captivity and power of the devil; for he seeketh that all men might be miserable like unto himself" (2 Nephi 2:27).

Even though all the answers we seek, or the choices we make, don't necessarily have eternal consequences attached to them, the pattern established in arriving at them will. Thus the great test of mortality is essentially a test of spiritual integrity. Ultimately there are no right answers that are not sustained by right reasons. "Beware lest any man spoil you through philosophy and vain deceit, after the tradition of men," warned the apostle Paul (Colossians 2:8). It need be clearly understood that neither philosophy nor the traditions of men, even when in harmony with revealed truth, is an acceptable source for those truths which all must know by the Spirit of revelation. All that comes from God must come through the channels ordained by God, for "every plant, which my heavenly Father hath not planted, shall be rooted up" (Matthew 15:13).

In like manner Peter reminds us that "no prophecy of the scripture is of any private interpretation" (2 Peter 1:20). There are no private doctrines, no inner circle of elect who alone are entitled to know the truths of salvation. All saving truths are in the public domain with every child of God having equal right to possess them.

Thus it is the common lot of all, and particularly of those who are alive to the things of the Spirit, to search for answers. The command to search the scriptures is theirs, as is the responsibility to "be ready always to give an answer to every man that asketh you a reason of the hope that is in you" (1 Peter 3:15). Most of us will be parents, we will have friends who are not Latter-day Saints, we will serve as missionaries, we will be called on to speak in various meetings, and we will hold teaching and leadership positions. Indeed, we hope to spend the better part of our lives sharing our faith with others. Because of that we spend a great deal of time teaching each other—more so than any other religious denomination on earth. That is by divine design. While the Church was still in its infancy the Lord said, "I give unto you a commandment that you shall teach one another the doctrine of the kingdom" (D&C 88:77). Those who are diligent in so doing have the promise that the grace or power of the Lord will sustain them (see D&C 88:78). To assure that there would be order in all of this, the Lord said, "Appoint among yourselves a teacher, and let not all be spokesmen at once; but let one speak at a time and let all listen unto his sayings, that when all have spoken that all may be edified of all, and that every man may have an equal privilege" (D&C 88:122). From the writings of Paul, we find that this was also the practice of the Saints in the meridian Church. To the Corinthian Saints he said, "Ye may all prophesy [meaning teach, reprove, admonish, or comfort] one by one, that all may learn, and all may be comforted" (1 Corinthians 14:31).

As to the matter of who has the right to answer questions, only the man who stands at the head of the Church or those acting under his direction have the right to speak for the Church. That does not mean, however, that everyone else is to remain mute. By revelation parents are commanded to teach the gospel to their children (see D&C 68:25–28), we are all charged to share the gospel with those not of our faith (see D&C 88:81), and we have a covenant obligation to teach one another (see D&C 88:77).

Some teachers have held that they have no right to do more in answering questions than quote what someone in a position of authority has said. Two assumptions are associated with such a course, both of which are false. The first is that gospel understanding comes from being called to a particular office or position. The second fallacious assumption is that when we quote someone in a respected position, we are excused from any responsibility to square what they have said with gospel principles and the standard works. If we are not able to evaluate the reliability of a quotation, there is good reason to question whether we should use it.

It should also be observed that there are many questions to which no answer has been given. When the meridian Twelve asked Christ when he was going to restore the kingdom of Israel, he responded that it was not for them to know either the times or the seasons in which that would take place (see Acts 1:6–7). When Joseph Smith asked to know when Christ would return, he was told that if he should live to the age of eighty-five he would see the face of the Son of Man (the meaning of which statement he did not understand) and that he was to quit troubling the Lord on the matter (see D&C 130:14–15). Some question marks are necessary in gospel study. Further, we are not without room in this Church for good people to hold some differences of opinion. "It does not prove that a man is not a good man because he errs in doctrine" (Smith, *History of the Church*, 5:340). It is pure silliness to argue that because someone was wrong on one matter he or she must be held suspect on all others. Credibility does not require infallibility. Surely we can have the good sense to allow someone to be in error on a matter or two and still hold him or her in high esteem. It is the system of heaven to dispense its treasures line upon line, precept upon precept. Among other things, this means that our generation ought to be able to improve upon the doctrinal understanding of the previous generations. If we are continuing the journey they started, we ought to be a bit closer to the top of Mount Zion and our view ought to be a bit better. If God has "many great and important things" to reveal to this people, surely we are obligated to prepare ourselves to receive them (Article of Faith 9).

This book is structured in a question-and-answer format. The questions are typical of those asked in a college religion class or a missionary zone conference. The answers are deliberately brief and for the most part are confined to the scriptures. They are intended to be the kind of answers that can be conveniently carried in one's head rather than stored in a filing cabinet or a reference book. No claim is made that they are the best possible answers, but it is hoped that they are good answers. It is further hoped that this work will also respond effectively to the question of how one finds answers and how one discerns good answers or good doctrine from bad.

ACKNOWLEDGMENTS

Special thanks to Margaret Christine Robertson, who did all the tedious things required to prepare a manuscript for publication and who made many helpful suggestions along the way. Thanks also to my brother Mark for his reading of the manuscript and to my friend and colleague Robert L. Miller, whose suggestions and experience are greatly valued. Suzanne Brady represented Deseret Book in her usual pleasant and insightful way. Good people are a great help.

CHAPTER ONE

TO HONEST SEEKERS
OF TRUTH

Y OU ARE NOW IN THE PRESENCE of the Holy Ghost," Elder
Hugh B. Brown of the Quorum of the Twelve testified to the
large group of young missionaries who sat before him. "And when
you go back to your digs tonight, I want you to write your parents
and tell them that you have felt his presence."

The moment Elder Brown told us we were in the presence of
the Holy Ghost, we knew it and could say in our hearts, "Yes, I
know that I am." Yet, most of us, inexperienced in the things of
the Spirit, would not have known what it was that we were expe-
riencing without the help of an able and experienced guide. It is a
wonderful blessing, as we seek to grow in the things of the Spirit,
to have an experienced mentor at our side. That has been my
blessing at various periods of my life and one for which I am very
grateful. I think particularly of my father, grandfathers, and mission president. They were visionary men who knew how to pray
and how to get answers. From them I learned the most important

lessons of my life. This volume seeks to share the lessons and the principles I learned from them. They were master teachers, and to the extent that this work reflects light and truth, the credit is theirs. As to anything that does not measure up to that standard, the responsibility is mine and the shame is that I was not a better student. Of greater importance, however, is that I am still a student and revel in the opportunity to improve my views and increase my understanding. Whether student or teacher, our obligation is to discover truth and to share the truth we discover.

WITH REAL INTENT

To find the truth we must first desire to find the truth. Far too often we ask questions to seek confirmation for something we have already chosen to believe or a course of action we are unwilling to change. Often we keep refining and re-asking our questions until we hear what we want to hear. Contrast such a course with this statement by Elder Bruce R. McConkie:

"I often think as I go around the Church and preach in various meetings that it just does not make a snap of the fingers difference to me what I am talking about. I do not care what I talk about. All I am concerned with is getting in tune with the Spirit and expressing the thoughts, in the best language and way that I can, that are implanted there by the power of the Spirit. The Lord knows what a congregation needs to hear, and he has provided a means to give that revelation to every preacher and every teacher.

"We do not create the doctrines of the gospel. People who ask questions about the gospel, a good portion of the time, are looking for an answer that sustains a view they have expressed. They want to justify a conclusion that they have reached instead of looking for the ultimate truth in the field. Once again, it does not make one snap of the fingers difference to me what the doctrines of the Church are. I cannot create a doctrine. I cannot originate a concept of eternal truth. The only thing I ought to be concerned with is learning what the Lord thinks about a doctrine. If I ask a question of someone to learn something, I ought *not* to be seeking for a confirmation of a view that I have expressed. I ought to be seeking knowledge and wisdom. It should not make any difference to me whether the doctrine is on the right hand or on the left. My sole interest and my sole concern would be to find out what the Lord thinks on the subject" ("Foolishness of Teaching," 8).

Speaking at the funeral of Elder McConkie, Elder Boyd K. Packer observed: "He could not measure what ought to be said and how it ought to be said by [asking], 'What will people think?' Would his sermons leave any uncomfortable? Would his bold declarations irritate some in the Church? Would they inspire the critics to rush to their anvils and hammer out more 'fiery darts' as the scriptures call them?

"Would his manner of delivery offend? Would his forthright declarations, in content or in manner of presentation, drive some learned investigators away? Would he be described as insensitive or overbearing?

"Would his warnings and condemnations of evil undo the careful work of others whose main intent was to have the world 'think well of the Church'? Perhaps it was given to other men to measure their words in that way, but it was not given to him.

"We have talked of this. And when he was tempted to change, the Spirit would withdraw a distance and there would come that deep loneliness known only to those who have enjoyed close association with the Spirit, only to find on occasion that it moves away. He could stand what the critics might say and what enemies might do, but he could not stand that.

"He would be driven to his knees to beg forgiveness and plead for the renewal of that companionship with the Spirit which the scriptures promise can be constant. Then he would learn once again that what was true of Holy Men of God who spake in ancient times applied to him as well. He was to speak as he was moved upon by the Holy Spirit. What matter if it sounded like Bruce R. McConkie, so long as the Lord approved. I knew him well enough to know all of that" (Salt Lake City, Utah, 23 April 1985, 6–7).

In the realm of gospel answers, we generally find what we want. If we want justification for a particular course of action, we often will search until we find it. If we want to defend some idea, we may filter out anything that does not sustain it. And if we want to discover the mind and will of the Lord, we generally find that also. We cannot inquire of the heavens with real intent and a sincere heart if we have already determined what we will accept as an answer. What must be understood is that it is "counted evil unto a man, if he shall pray and not with real intent of heart; yea, and it profiteth him nothing, for God receiveth none such" (Moroni 7:9).

BE BELIEVING

The pattern of scripture is that God reveals that which those to whom the revelation is initially given are willing to believe. When Nephi sought to see the vision shown his father, the angel who acted as his mentor asked, "Believest thou that thy father saw the tree of which he hath spoken?" (1 Nephi 11:4). Only Nephi's affirmative response allowed him to proceed. Before the Lord manifested himself to the brother of Jared, He asked, "Believest thou the words which I shall speak?" (Ether 3:11). It was clearly expected that the commitment to believe preceded the explanation of what he was to believe. We find this same spirit in the story of Aaron teaching Lamoni's father. When Aaron asked, "Believest thou that there is a God?" the king responded, "If now thou sayest there is a God, behold I will believe." And again the king said, "I will believe thy words" (Alma 22:7, 11). Still again we find this spirit in Alma's often quoted discourse in which he likens the word of God to a seed: "Blessed is he that believeth in the word of God, and is baptized without stubbornness of heart, yea, *without being brought to know the word*, or even compelled to know, before they will believe" (Alma 32:16; emphasis added).

The idea that we are expected to accept and believe doctrines, or divine answers in any form, even before we have heard them, does not make good sense to the world. Upon examination, however, it makes perfect sense to those of the household of faith. It is simply the commitment to accept truth, without attempting to color or fashion it to our own liking. If an answer comes from the Lord, from holy writ, from one of his servants, or by the quiet whisperings of the Spirit, we accept it without having to be argued into submission. The instruction and promise given those of the household of faith is to "trust in the Lord with all thine heart; and lean not unto thine own understanding. In all thy ways acknowledge him, and he shall direct thy paths" (Proverbs 3:5–6). "Despise not, and wonder not, but hearken unto the words of the Lord, and ask the Father in the name of Jesus for what things soever ye shall stand in need. Doubt not, but be believing, and begin as in times of old, and come unto the Lord with all your heart, and work out your own salvation with fear and trembling before him" (Mormon 9:27).

Beware of the Precepts of Men

Every truth of salvation, that is, every doctrine or principle that we must accept and live in order to be saved, was taught to us before we were born. We came into this life knowing but having forgotten these sacred truths. When these truths are declared to us we are expected to remember and respond to them. This singular truth is announced in a variety of ways in scripture. For instance, consider these words from the Prophet Joseph Smith: "Here is the agency of man, and here is the condemnation of man; because that which was from the beginning [known to us in the premortal life] is plainly manifest unto them [the recall is powerful and clear], and they receive not the light. And every man whose spirit receiveth not the light is under condemnation" (D&C 93:31–32). Well might it be asked, What is it that blurs spiritual recall or the recognition of truth? To which this revelation responds: "Light and truth forsake that evil one. . . . And that wicked one cometh and taketh away light and truth, through disobedience, from the children of men, and because of the tradition of their fathers" (D&C 93:37–39).

The two great opponents of light and truth are thus identified as "disobedience" and "the tradition of their fathers." To communicate with the Spirit, we must be in tune with the Spirit. The experience of anyone who has served as a missionary will attest that there are many who "desire to know the truth in part, but not all," for as the Lord said, "they are not right before me and must needs repent" (D&C 49:2). These people love the spirit that the missionaries bring into their homes. They thrill at the truths of the plan of salvation as they are unfolded to them. They enjoy that sweet spirit of recall as the elders or sisters restore to them knowledge and feelings long lost to them. Yet they struggle to find the courage or the necessary discipline to accord their lives with gospel standards, and so they seek excuses and act as if they are uncertain about the truthfulness of the principles presented to them. They remind us of Amulek when he said: "I never have known much of the ways of the Lord, and his mysteries and marvelous power. I said I never had known much of these things; but behold, I mistake, for I have seen much of his mysteries and his marvelous power; yea, even in the preservation of the lives of this people. Nevertheless, I did harden my heart, for I was called many times and I would not hear; therefore I knew concerning these things, yet I would not know; therefore I went on rebelling against God, in the wickedness of my heart" (Alma 10:5–6).

Leaving the matter of disobedience as one of the two great blocks to spiritual understanding, let us turn our attention to the second, "the tradition of their fathers." In the First Vision the Lord described apostate Christendom, saying, "They teach for doctrines the commandments of men, having a form of godliness, but they deny the power thereof" (Joseph Smith–History 1:19). Neither salvation nor any of the truths of salvation have their origin in the mind of man. In his description of the false churches of the last days, Nephi warns of those who teach with their own learning while denying the Holy Ghost. "They wear stiff necks and high heads; yea, and because of pride, and wickedness, and abominations, and whoredoms, they have all gone astray save it be a few, who are the humble followers of Christ; nevertheless, they are led, that in many instances they do err because they are taught by the precepts of men" (2 Nephi 28:14). Having considered the havoc that such a course plays with the principles of truth, Nephi warns, "Cursed is he that putteth his trust in man, or maketh flesh his arm, or shall hearken unto the precepts of men, save their precepts shall be given by the power of the Holy Ghost" (2 Nephi 28:31).

Two simple keys unlock understanding where gospel truths are concerned. The first is the verity that every revelation from heaven carries within itself the evidence of its own origin. That is the spirit of truth. President Marion G. Romney stated the principle thus: "No person is, nor can he be, justified in rejecting these teachings and commandments, which have been revealed by the Lord, on the basis that he does not know they are true, because everything the Lord does or says has within itself the evidence of its own authenticity, and every person is divinely endowed with the means to discover that evidence and know for himself that it is true" (in Conference Report, April 1976, 120–21). Teaching this same principle, Joseph Smith said that truth tastes good. "I can taste the principles of eternal life," he said, "and so can you. They are given to me by the revelations of Jesus Christ; and I know that when I tell you these words of eternal life as they are given to me, you taste them, and I know that you believe them. You say honey is sweet, and so do I. I can also taste the spirit of eternal life. I know it is good; and when I tell you of these things which were given me by inspiration of the Holy Spirit, you are bound to receive them as sweet, and rejoice more and more" (*Teachings of the Prophet Joseph Smith*, 355).

The second key by which we obtain a sure knowledge of gospel truths is in applying, or living, those truths. A true testimony of any principle comes only from living it. A testimony of tithing comes by paying tithing, a testimony of the Word of Wisdom comes by living the Word of Wisdom, and so forth. Teaching this principle, the Savior said, "If any man will do his [the Father's] will, he shall know of the doctrine, whether it be of God, or whether I speak of myself" (John 7:17).

SEARCH THE SCRIPTURES

"Be careful that you teach not for the word of God the commandments of men, nor the doctrines of men, nor the ordinances of men, inasmuch as you are God's messengers," stated Brigham Young. "Study the word of God, and preach it and not your opinions, for no man's opinion is worth a straw. Advance no principle but what you can prove, for one scriptural proof is worth ten thousand opinions" (Smith, *History of the Church*, 3:395–96).

It hardly needs to be said that the search for spiritual answers centers in the thoughtful and prayerful study of the scriptures. What is not as well understood, however, is that all scripture is not of equal worth. The voice of God to modern prophets must of necessity supersede that which he said to those of an earlier day. We read both the Old and New Testaments by the light of modern revelation. To refuse that light is to read in the dark and to place ourselves and those we teach under condemnation. "And your minds in times past have been darkened," the Lord said, "because of unbelief, and because you have treated lightly the things you have received [namely the Book of Mormon, the restoration of the priesthood, and some eighty-three other revelations now found in the Doctrine and Covenants]—which vanity and unbelief have brought the whole church under condemnation. And this condemnation resteth upon the children of Zion, even all. And they shall remain under this condemnation until they repent and remember the new covenant, even the Book of Mormon and the former commandments which I have given them, not only to say, but to do according to that which I have written—that they may bring forth fruit meet for their Father's kingdom; otherwise there remaineth a scourge and judgment to be poured out upon the children of Zion" (D&C 84:54–58). In contrast, there is a special endowment of spiritual knowledge promised to those who place their trust in the revelations of the Restoration (see D&C 5:16; 18:2–5).

It is popular to say that we should read scripture and not commentaries on scripture. Certainly the scriptures should be the focal point of our study, yet there is not a soul alive whose understanding of scripture will not be enhanced by helpful commentary on it. Were this not the case we would not have Sunday School classes, Relief Society lessons, and quorum instruction for priesthood bearers. We would not have the seminary program, nor would we have institutes of religion. Much that we have in the scriptures is prophetic commentary on other scripture. The instruction of scripture is that we teach each other in both the spoken and written word. "As all have not faith," the Lord said, "seek ye diligently and teach one another words of wisdom; yea, seek ye out of the best books words of wisdom; seek learning, even by study and also by faith" (D&C 88:118). We are to seek learning from both the best books and the best people. As the wisdom of heaven ought to dictate what books we read, so it ought to dictate what people we listen to when we seek understanding of heaven-sent principles. We don't have to agree with everything in a book for it to be a good book, and a man doesn't have to be right on everything to be worth listening to. There is much we can learn from each other. The commandment is that we teach one another the doctrines of the kingdom (see D&C 88:77). The rule of thumb here is that you "trust no one to be your teacher nor your minister, except he be a man of God, walking in his ways and keeping his commandments" (Mosiah 23:14).

ASK, AND IT SHALL BE GIVEN

When Nephi's brothers said they could not understand the things their father had told them, Nephi asked if they had inquired of the Lord. They said they had not because "the Lord maketh no such thing known unto us." "Do ye not remember," Nephi responded, "the things which the Lord hath said?—If ye will not harden your hearts, and ask me in faith, believing that ye shall receive, with diligence in keeping my commandments, surely these things shall be made known unto you" (1 Nephi 15:9, 11). We assume the text he quoted came from the brass plates. The fact that it has no counterpart in the Old Testament suggests that it was among the plain and precious things taken from that record. In the Sermon on the Mount, Christ, directing himself to his disciples, said, "Ask, and it shall be given you; seek, and ye shall find; knock, and it shall be opened unto you: for every one that asketh receiveth; and he that seeketh findeth; and to him that knocketh it shall be opened" (Matthew 7:7–8).

James repeated this same injunction, telling us that if we seek wisdom, we should ask God, who "giveth to all men liberally, and upbraideth not," meaning they would not be reproached for so doing because God is a generous giver (James 1:5). Other texts make it clear that though God is anxious to bless his earthly family with light and knowledge, he will not give unto dogs that which is holy nor cast pearls before swine (see Matthew 7:6). The invitation to ask of God with the promise of an answer is given frequently in scripture. It is common, however, for this promise to contain appropriate modifiers. It was not intended that the blessings or wisdom of heaven be given to those who would misuse them or who have not properly prepared to receive them. We are told to ask only for that which is "expedient" (D&C 88:64), "good" (Moroni 7:26), or "right" (Mosiah 4:21). We are warned against asking for that which might be "amiss" or for that which we wish to consume upon our lusts (James 4:3). We are told we must pray with an honest heart, real intent, and faith (see Moroni 10:4). Further, we are to "keep [God's] commandments" (1 John 3:22), be believing (see Enos 1:8, 15), and pray always to the Father in the name of the Son (see Moroni 10:4; 3 Nephi 18:19–20).

"The best way to obtain truth and wisdom," Joseph Smith said, "is not to ask it from books, but to go to God in prayer, and obtain divine teaching" (*Teachings of the Prophet Joseph Smith*, 191). As Latter-day Saints, we have no doctrine that is not rooted in the principle of revelation. All true religion is revealed religion. Thus if a principle or doctrine does not come by way of revelation, that principle or doctrine is not a part of our religion. It may be a good principle, and it may be a great blessing to us, but if revelation is not its source, it is not a matter of faith with us.

The principle of revelation must be immediate and personal with each member of the Church. No one can be saved by a revelation given to someone else. That is not to suggest that every principle must be revealed anew to each member of the Church. It is, however, to say that the truthfulness of the doctrines of salvation must be learned and confirmed by the same Spirit by which they were originally given. All faithful Saints are expected to share that experience. Prayer is not an option to a Latter-day Saint; it is a commandment. We are also commanded to have the Spirit of revelation. After our baptism, hands were laid upon our head and the command given: "Receive ye the Holy Ghost." We cannot receive the Holy Ghost without receiving revelations (see Smith, *Teachings of the Prophet Joseph Smith*, 328).

Having thus received the gift of the Holy Ghost, we have also received the responsibility to grow up into it. Thus the scriptures speak of our receiving "a fulness of the Holy Ghost" (D&C 109:15). To do so is to develop the power of discernment. That is what Moroni was speaking of when he said that "by the power of the Holy Ghost ye may know the truth of all things" (Moroni 10:5). That is why the Lord, when asked if we should study the Apocrypha, responded: "The Spirit manifesteth truth; and whoso is enlightened by the Spirit shall obtain benefit therefrom; and whoso receiveth not by the Spirit, cannot be benefited" (D&C 91:4–6).

In Righteousness and in Truth

To what tests can we subject an answer to a gospel question or a revelation to assure that it is correct?

First, we should ask, "What is its purpose?" Let me illustrate. Missionaries meet many people who profess to have had spiritual experiences. How do we determine which are genuine and which are counterfeit? The answer is surprisingly simple. If their experience justifies them in rejecting the message of the Restoration—including our testimony that Joseph Smith is a prophet, the Book of Mormon is true, that the authority to baptize has been restored again to the earth, that living prophets are necessary, and that it is necessary to receive the sealing blessings of the temple—we need not hesitate in concluding that their experience has come from an untoward source. On the other hand, if their experience opens their hearts to the message of the Restoration and the covenants, obligations, and sacrifices that are associated with it, we can know for a surety that it is of God. True revelations or spiritual experiences do not place a person in opposition to the doctrines, purposes, or objectives of the Church and kingdom of God. "He that is not with me is against me," the Lord has said (Matthew 12:30; Luke 11:23).

Second, we should ask further, "Does it edify?" "That which doth not edify is not of God, and is darkness" (D&C 50:23). Again, let me illustrate. In stake leadership meetings, my father, Elder Bruce R. McConkie, used to enjoy question-and-answer sessions with priesthood leaders. Any appropriate gospel question was welcome. I remember one such session in which someone sought support for an idea that is not good doctrine and yet is still a popular part of Latter-day Saint lore. In responding to the question, my father asked, "What good could possibly come from teaching such a thing?" His question establishes a standard for sound doctrine—its spirit and purpose must be positive.

The Spirit of the Lord and all doctrines that trace to it must edify. The principles of salvation have no kinship with hopelessness, depression, or grief. They are not dark, cold, or unfeeling. Truth always sustains the idea of a just and merciful God. If a principle does not lift, encourage, inspire, or edify it certainly does not come from God and cannot be considered doctrine. Perhaps the two most often used words to describe the presence of the Holy Ghost are "peace" and "joy." In scripture the gospel is often referred to as "glad tidings," or "glad tidings of great joy" (Mosiah 3:3; Alma 13:22; D&C 31:3; 128:19). Good doctrine will always carry a positive and uplifting spirit.

Third, we should ask, "Is it born of obscurity?" Our understanding of the principles of salvation will never depend on an obscure scriptural text or some little-known discourse by one of the Brethren. The principles of salvation are taught plainly and repetitiously in the scriptures. There are no hidden or private doctrines that are the exclusive providence of an inner circle of faithful souls. There is but one plan of salvation. Its doctrines and ordinances are the same for all.

It is true that some things are more sacred than others and are thus spoken of with greater constraint and care. Yet, the Prophet explained, "God hath not revealed anything to Joseph, but what He will make known unto the Twelve, and even the least Saint may know all things as fast as he is able to bear them" (*Teachings of the Prophet Joseph Smith,* 149).

Fourth, we should ask, "Does it require obedience to the laws and ordinances of the gospel?" In the early history of the Church, at a time when Church members were often troubled by false spirits, the Lord gave the following instruction: "I will give unto you a pattern in all things, that ye may not be deceived; for Satan is abroad in the land, and he goeth forth deceiving the nations—wherefore he that prayeth, whose spirit is contrite, the same is accepted of me if he obey mine ordinances. He that speaketh, whose spirit is contrite, whose language is meek and edifieth, the same is of God if he obey mine ordinances" (D&C 52:14–16). The word *ordinance*, as used in this text, refers to all the laws, statutes, and covenants associated with the restored gospel. It is not confined to our compliance with such prescribed rituals as baptism and eternal marriage.

Finally, we should ask, "Is it in harmony with scripture and with the voice of our living prophets?" The Lord gave this instruction in the Doctrine and Covenants: "And again, he that trembleth under my power shall be made strong, and shall bring forth fruits of praise and wisdom, according to the revelations and truths which I have given you. And again, he that is overcome and bringeth not forth fruits, even according to this pattern, is not of me. Wherefore, by this pattern ye shall know the spirits in all cases under the whole heavens" (D&C 52:17–19).

Paul told us that "no man speaking by the Spirit of God calleth Jesus accursed" (1 Corinthians 12:3). That is to say, it is absolutely impossible for a man to enjoy the companionship of the Spirit of the Lord or the Holy Ghost and at the same time speak against Christ or his doctrines. Expanding on that principle, we could say in like manner that no one could speak against Joseph Smith, the Book of Mormon, or the revelations of the Restoration and at the same time enjoy the companionship of the Spirit. Thus we find Moroni saying, "He that will contend against the word of the Lord, let him be accursed; and he that shall deny these things, let him be accursed" (Ether 4:8).

LET EVERY MAN BEWARE

Years ago I read a book about a man who had been a prominent leader in the Church. In doing so I was quite surprised to learn about his attitude on a number of things. His feelings on these matters were not in accord with what I understood the standards of the Church to be. I mentioned the matter to my father, from whom I then learned a valuable lesson. Everyone, he explained, is responsible for what he believes and for what he chooses not to believe. That someone in a position of leadership made some poor choices in what he believed or did in no way excused the same kind of choices on my part. Each of us, my father reminded me, will stand alone at the Day of Judgment.

"We consider that God has created man with a mind capable of instruction," Joseph Smith taught, "and a faculty which may be enlarged in proportion to the heed and diligence given to the light communicated from heaven to the intellect; and that the nearer man approaches perfection, the clearer are his views, and the greater his enjoyments, till he has overcome the evils of his life and lost every desire for sin" (*Teachings of the Prophet Joseph Smith*, 51). It is a personal journey of which the Prophets speaks, one not necessarily associated with positions of leadership or other forms of prominence. Indeed, every member of the Church has an equal responsibility to know and understand the truth. Similarly, each one has equal access to it. We were all taught the gospel long before we were born, we all receive the same promise of direction and companionship when we receive the gift of the Holy Ghost, and we all receive the same endowment of power from on high when we go through the temple. Further, we all have the same right to approach our Father in Heaven in prayer, and we have all been given the same scriptures. Wearied by my endless questions, my father once said to me, "Look, Junior, you have the same sources available to you that I have available to me." The promise of the Lord to reveal the mysteries of heaven has nothing to do with office, position, station in society, or gender. It has everything to do with the desires of our hearts and our willingness to love and serve the Lord (see D&C 76:5–10). Thus in a revelation warning that there will be both false doctrines and hypocrites in the Church, the Lord charged "every man" to "beware lest he do that which is not in truth and righteousness before me" (D&C 50:9).

CHAPTER TWO

QUESTIONS COMMONLY ASKED BY THOSE NOT OF OUR FAITH

Why did the Lord wait so long to restore the gospel?

Why did the gospel have to be restored in the United States?

Why do we need the Book of Mormon when we have the Bible?

We have the scriptures, so why do we need a living prophet? Aren't the leaders of the various churches the same as prophets?

Why was it necessary for the Church to practice plural marriage?

Will smoking or an occasional drink keep someone out of heaven?

Why were blacks denied the priesthood for so long?

Why does a loving God allow so much suffering and sorrow?

Why do some critics of the Church say that Mormons aren't Christians?

Why are Latter-day Saints so unchristian as to suppose that The Church of Jesus Christ of Latter-day Saints is the only true church?

Why is rebaptism necessary in joining the Mormon church?

WHEN WE AS LATTER-DAY SAINTS respond to questions about our faith, we do so in the hope that those asking the questions will be impressed with the truths that are ours and seek to unite themselves with us. It is never our purpose to give offense. It's converts we want, not antagonists. The spirit of kindness and gentleness should attend our message, not a spirit of contention. We cannot expect, however, that our message will always be received in the same spirit in which we seek to deliver it. The scriptures describe the word of the Lord as being both "powerful" and "sharper than a two-edged sword," even "to the dividing asunder of both joints and marrow" (D&C 11:2). Joseph Smith was promised that his name, which is inextricably tied to the message that is ours, would be known for "good and evil," meaning that it would be "both good and evil spoken of among all people" (Joseph Smith–History 1:33).

Until the day in which Satan is bound, the truths of the gospel will never go unopposed. Christ was unable to deliver his message without giving offense, and he promised the Twelve, whom he had specially called as messengers of that same gospel, that they would be "hated of all nations" for his "name's sake" (Joseph Smith–Matthew 1:7) and be killed because of the message they bore. Such was the lot of "most of the Lord's anointed in ancient times" (D&C 135:3), and such was the lot of Joseph and Hyrum Smith, who stood at the head of the dispensation of the gospel we have been called to declare. At the present time, few people court martyrdom in joining the Church or in answering questions about it. Yet in many situations some Latter-day Saints have an anxiety about presenting our message in a way that will be acceptable to others. This anxiety frequently manifests itself in efforts to impress people with Latter-day Saint celebrities or programs and activities the Church sponsors rather than calling attention to beliefs that might be deemed peculiar. We also find this anxiety manifest in exaggerated efforts to convince people that "we are just like them." The problem with such an approach ought to be obvious but apparently is not. Infatuation with either people or programs cannot engender the kind of faith our pioneer forefathers had or that we need to achieve our destiny. If we succeed in our efforts to convince people that we are really "just like them," we will at the same time have convinced them that we have nothing to offer them that they do not have or cannot obtain in the system of worship that is presently theirs. Of greater concern is the possibility that we may in the process convince ourselves that this is the case.

What, then, is it that we want to do in answering questions from those not of our faith? May I suggest that nothing more is needed than to give simple, straightforward answers that are attractive to the Spirit of the Lord. That Spirit will sustain the goodness and truthfulness of the doctrines we are teaching. We would do well to answer questions from the revelations of the Restoration rather than trying to hide behind Bible texts. President Marion G. Romney observed: "In each dispensation, . . . the Lord has revealed anew the principles of the gospel. So that while the records of past dispensations, insofar as they are uncorrupted, testify to the truths of the gospel, still each dispensation has had revealed in its day sufficient truth to guide the people of the new dispensation, independent of the records of the past" ("Glorious Promise," 2).

There are a number of good reasons for this practice: First, it emphasizes that which is distinctly and uniquely ours. Again, if we don't have something that makes us distinct and unique, why all the fuss? Second, there is nothing we can do that is more attractive to the Spirit than being true to the revelations of the Restoration. These revelations speak for themselves; they testify of their own truthfulness. Third, the experience of missionaries who use this approach continually shows that people are innately more believing and raise fewer objections when we stand on our own ground instead of attempting to find common ground. Fourth, it is the best way to avoid the spirit of contention which often attends discussions about what the Bible really means. Let me illustrate.

QUESTION

Why did the Lord wait so long to restore the gospel?

ANSWER

Even a cursory knowledge of history from the time of Christ to the time of the Restoration makes it plain that God, in wisdom, could not have restored the gospel a moment before he did. One cannot rush the time of planting or the time of harvest. To impatiently sow new seed during winter storms will not hasten the day of germination. Let us briefly consider the time of the Great Apostasy and the time of the Restoration.

No exact date can be given as to when the purity of the gospel and the authority of the priesthood were lost. In the Old World it would have been after the death of the apostles and long before the Council of Nicaea in A.D. 325. The New World dispensation of the gospel, as recorded in the Book of Mormon, lasted for four hundred years after the visit of Christ among the Nephites. Perhaps it lasted longer with them than among other of the lost tribes of Israel visited by the resurrected Christ, and perhaps not; we are without any knowledge to that effect (see 3 Nephi 16:1–4). In any event, if we are going to lay claim to the fulfillment of the prophecies of a restoration of all things in the last days, we are bound to the position that these same things were universally lost. Thus, as nearly as we can tell, there was a period of approximately fourteen hundred years in which the gospel and the priesthood were lost to the inhabitants of the earth. Thus the question, Why did the Lord allow such an extended period to pass before he caused the gospel to be restored?

History affords us a clear answer to our question. Consider the struggle associated with freeing the Bible from its papal prison and placing it in the hands of the common man. "'All reading of the scriptures, all discussion within one's own doors concerning faith, the sacraments, the papal or other religious matter, was forbidden under penalty of death,' writes [J. L.] Motley in *The Rise of the Dutch Republic* [Burts' ed.]. 'The edicts were no dead letter. The fires were kept constantly supplied with human fuel by monks who knew the art of burning reformers better than that of arguing with them. The scaffold was the most conclusive of syllogisms, and used upon all occasions' [1:68]." Continuing his account, Motley tells us that "'the number of Netherlanders who were burned, strangled, beheaded, or buried alive, in obedience to his [Charles V's] edicts, and for the offense of reading the scriptures, or looking askance at a graven image, or of ridiculing the actual presence of the body and blood of Christ in a wafer, has been placed as high as one hundred thousand by distinguished authorities, and has never been put at a lower mark than fifty thousand' [1:99]" (Smith, *Doctrines of Salvation*, 3:186).

President Joseph Fielding Smith also wrote that "the English chronicler, Henry Kneighton, many years before had expressed the prevailing notion about the reading of the scriptures, when he denounced the general reading of the Bible, lamenting 'lest the jewel of the church hitherto the exclusive property of the clergy and divines, should be made common to the laity.' Archbishop Arundel, in England, had issued an enactment that 'no part of the scriptures in English should be read, either in public or in private, or be thereafter translated, under pain of the greater excommunication.' . . .

"In the reign of Henry VIII, the reading of the Bible by the common people, or those who were not of the privileged class, had been prohibited by act of parliament, and men were burned at the stake in England as well as in the Netherlands and elsewhere for having even fragments of the scriptures in their possession" (*Doctrines of Salvation*, 3:185–86).

The point here is that this was hardly the climate that would welcome the Book of Mormon.

The struggle for religious freedom did not come easily, even in the New World. Vermont did not enjoy a separation of church and state until 1807, Connecticut until 1818, New Hampshire until 1819, and Maine until 1820. Massachusetts was the last of the states to divorce herself from such an entanglement with religion, not doing so until 1833.

The manner in which those who embraced the restored gospel were persecuted attests that the Restoration could not have taken place any earlier than it did. It survived in the Americas only because the powers of heaven intervened to protect the Saints and because there was a place of refuge of sufficient size, distance, and difficulty to reach to which the Saints could flee for protection. Such a place did not exist in the Old World. Nevertheless, it still "cost the best blood of the nineteenth century" (D&C 135:6), for Joseph and Hyrum Smith were martyred in Carthage, Illinois, and thousands of the Saints died before the Lord's people found safety in the West.

Perhaps it should be noted that the question of why there was such an extended time before the gospel was restored is not entirely peculiar to Latter-day Saints. Protestants might likewise ask why the Lord allowed sixteen hundred years of confusion before making clear to us through Martin Luther and others what we are told today is the one and only system of salvation. And then the attendant questions, What is to become of all those in that interim period who didn't adhere to the modern system? Wouldn't a just God be required to save them by adherence to the Catholic system, given that he hadn't bothered to send anyone to show the true way in their lifetimes? Or, if we are to argue that salvation could be found in the Catholic system before the Reformation, why not after it?

QUESTION

Why did the gospel have to be restored in the United States?

ANSWER

Many people throughout the world resent the United States and take offense at the idea that they must accept an American religion to be saved. That is unfortunate, because it is not Americanism we have been commissioned to take to the nations of the earth but the restored gospel. To the extent we have associated it with an American culture, we have erred. Great effort is made to avoid this. Still the question remains, Why the United States? Our answer properly includes the following:

First, a nation fostering religious freedom and toleration was required, one in which there was a separation of church and state. For this reason alone at the time of Joseph Smith the Church could not have been organized anywhere in Europe.

Second, the host country for the Restoration had to be one from which emissaries would have the freedom to carry its message to all other nations.

Third, the place of the Restoration had to be one to which the newly converted could, at least in its early stages, freely gather.

Fourth, the gospel had to be restored in a country of sufficient natural wealth that those who would bear the burden of sending missionaries by the hundreds of thousands to those of other nations could afford to do so.

Fifth, the plates from which the Book of Mormon was translated had been deposited, in the providence of God, in upstate New York.

When Nephi saw the marvelous dream that had been shown to his father, he learned about the destruction of his people by the Lamanites and how they would then scatter themselves throughout the continent. He was shown "a man among the Gentiles" (1 Nephi 13:12)—that is, someone from Europe—who would be wrought upon by the Spirit to discover the land once inhabited by Nephi's people. After this discovery, many would come to this land to escape the captivity of the Old World. Nephi was also shown what we know to be the Revolutionary War and how "the power of God" (1 Nephi 13:18) rested upon those fighting to maintain the Americas as a land of political and religious freedom. Having recounted these events, Nephi then gives a prophetic description of the history of the Bible. He tells how plain and precious parts were taken from it and how it would then go forth to "the nations of the Gentiles" (1 Nephi 13:29) and how many would stumble because of the things that had been taken away. He then tells the story of the coming forth of the Book of Mormon and the restoration of the gospel on the American continent (see 1 Nephi 12–14).

In short, then, the United States was formed for the purpose of providing a birthplace for the Restoration, a place from which its message and blessings could then be taken to all nations and all peoples.

QUESTION

Why do we need the Book of Mormon when we have the Bible?

ANSWER

Nephi, like many of the ancient prophets, was invited to see our day. He knew of the importance of the records he and his fellow prophets in the Americas were keeping and of the arguments that would be brought against them. Speaking for the Lord, he penned these words: "And because my words shall hiss forth— many of the Gentiles shall say: A Bible! A Bible! We have got a Bible, and there cannot be any more Bible. . . . Thou fool, that shall say: A Bible, we have got a Bible, and we need no more Bible. . . . Know ye not that there are more nations than one?

Know ye not that I, the Lord your God, have created all men, and that I remember those who are upon the isles of the sea; and that I rule in the heavens above and in the earth beneath; and I bring forth my word unto the children of men, yea, even upon all the nations of the earth? Wherefore murmur ye, because that ye shall receive more of my word? Know ye not that the testimony of two nations is a witness unto you that I am God, that I remember one nation like unto another? Wherefore, I speak the same words unto one nation like unto another. And when the two nations shall run together the testimony of the two nations shall run together also. . . . Wherefore, because that ye have a Bible ye need not suppose that it contains all my words; neither need ye suppose that I have not caused more to be written. For I command all men, both in the east and in the west, and in the north, and in the south, and in the islands of the sea, that they shall write the words which I speak unto them; for out of the books which shall be written I will judge the world, every man according to their works, according to that which is written" (2 Nephi 29:3–11).

Why a Book of Mormon? Because it gives us an independent witness that Jesus is the Christ, the literal Son of God, conceived by Mary "after the manner of the flesh" (1 Nephi 11:18). It is a powerful witness that Christ labored among men, was judged by them, and was slain upon a cross "for the sins of the world" (1 Nephi 11:33). It affirms that he rose again in an inseparable union of body and spirit, that he loosed the bands of death for all, and that thus he made it possible for those who take upon themselves his name to obtain eternal life, which is God's life (see Alma 11:40–41).

Why a Book of Mormon? Because it is the doctrinal foundation of the Church and the last great dispensation of the gospel before the return of Christ (see D&C 18:4–5).

Why a Book of Mormon? Because it is a witness of the truthfulness of the Bible. It both sustains its doctrines and constitutes a fulfillment of its prophecies (see D&C 20:11; 1 Nephi 13:40;

2 Nephi 2:11–12; 3; 27; 3 Nephi 16:15–20; Isaiah 29; Ezekiel 37:15–28; John 10:16; Revelation 14:6–7; Joseph Smith–History 1:27–54).

Why a Book of Mormon? Because God, who directed that we "prove all things" and "hold fast that which is good" (1 Thessalonians 5:21), gave us the book as tangible evidence that Joseph Smith is a prophet (see D&C 20:11). The Book of Mormon is to our dispensation what the testimony of the apostles and prophets who had seen the resurrected Christ and touched the wounds in his hands and feet were to those in the meridian of time.

Why a Book of Mormon? Because it is sure proof that God is the same yesterday, today, and forever (see D&C 20:11; 1 Nephi 10:17–19). As he spoke through prophets anciently, so he does today. As he sent angels to minister in his name in ancient times, so he does today. As he was a God of miracles in ages past, so he is today.

Why a Book of Mormon? Because a myriad of conflicting doctrines claim the Bible as their source—thus creating the need for a second book of scripture, one pure in its origin, from which the true meaning of the Bible can be obtained (see 2 Nephi 3:11–12).

Why a Book of Mormon? Because in the providence of God it has been ordained as the scriptural record that will touch the heart of scattered Israel and gather them to the faith and promises known to their ancient fathers (see Book of Mormon, title page).

Why a Book of Mormon? Because the common person can understand and interpret its doctrines with the same authority as the scholar. Thus all stand on common ground before God.

Why a Book of Mormon? Because it restores to us the "plain and precious" truths taken from the Bible by evil and designing men (1 Nephi 13:20–29, 40).

Why a Book of Mormon? Because it is the perfect test of spiritual integrity. Acceptance of the Book of Mormon requires the same faith that was necessary to accept Christ in the meridian of

time. As he was opposed by false traditions and a corrupt priesthood, so the Book of Mormon is opposed today. The doctrines are
the same, the opposition is the same, and the courage and faith
necessary to accept it are the same.

QUESTION

We have the scriptures, so why do we need a living prophet?
Aren't the leaders of the various churches the same as prophets?

ANSWER

Let us consider the second part of the question first. If by
prophet we mean someone who has the authority, as did the
ancients, to write scripture, the answer is no! The leaders of other
churches are not the same as prophets, nor do they claim to be. To
suggest otherwise would deny a basic tenet of traditional
Christianity, which holds that the canon of scripture is closed.

As to the question of why we need a prophet when we have
the scriptures, we might best answer by raising a few questions of
our own. If a man were to come among us with the wisdom, power,
and knowledge of Moses, why would people of faith and judgment
object? Or if God were going to speak today, as he once did from
Sinai, wouldn't we want to listen? Why would anyone who loves
scripture and hungers for truth object to the idea of a living
prophet?

Further, wouldn't we hold suspect those who refused to listen
to the voice of God in this day? I am aware of the argument that
God has chosen to speak to us today through scripture and not
through prophets, but I am equally aware that no prophet ever said
that. It has to be evident that the only possible reason people
wouldn't want to hear from a living prophet is the fear that he
might have something to say that they didn't want to hear. It is
almost as if we suppose that by not knowing something, we can
prevent its existence. Perhaps that gives some license to justify our

doing or our failing to do particular things, but the reality is that our refusal to listen to a particular truth will not negate or change that truth.

In the scriptures the prophet was the covenant spokesman. This means he had the authority to say, "Thus saith the Lord." The scriptures do not constitute the gospel; they are simply a record of some of the experiences known to those who had it. Scriptures are a great blessing to us, but they do not replace the need for a living voice to interpret them and to ensure that we make appropriate application of them. Such has ever been the role of the prophet. He has the authority to teach scripture, to interpret scripture, and to speak new scripture, thereby keeping the gospel as relevant to us as the ancient prophets did to those of their day.

QUESTION

Why was it necessary for the Church to practice plural marriage?

ANSWER

It stands to reason that the gospel of Jesus Christ embraces doctrines and practices that are offensive to the world. The world accepts only its own doctrines and its own churches. The idea that their Messiah was to be a suffering servant who would die an ignominious death on a Roman cross was anything but a doctrine that could be expected to be popular among the Jews. True doctrines do not appeal to those whose hearts are set upon the things of the world. The idea that God can speak, that revelation continues, and that Joseph Smith was a prophet in every sense that Moses and Isaiah were prophets, was and is highly offensive to the world. The doctrine of the plurality of wives was equally offensive, as has been the doctrine of who can and cannot hold the priesthood and the role of women in the Church. We may not be able to predict what doctrines those of the world will take offense at in the future, but we have every assurance that they will have cause for offense.

Ours is not a new church; ours is a restored Church. We have no doctrines that were not known to the Saints of dispensations past. The prophetic descriptions of our day describe a restoration of all things—meaning all pure doctrines and righteous practices of the Saints in dispensations past. The doctrine of plurality of wives came to the ancient prophets by the command of heaven and was restored to us in like manner (see D&C 132:40, 45). Our forefathers practiced plural marriage because God commanded them to do so. They did it under the direction of the prophet and were greatly blessed for doing so. When the prophet commanded that they cease the practice, they did so, in harmony with the same Spirit.

QUESTION

Will smoking or an occasional drink keep someone out of heaven?

ANSWER

It can be confidently said that in the kingdom of heaven there will be neither smoking nor drinking. The scriptures repeatedly declare that "no unclean thing" can enter into the presence of God (1 Nephi 10:21; 3 Nephi 27:19; Moses 6:57). All habits of any degree of uncleanness must be discarded before one obtains citizenship in that kingdom. Neither alcohol nor tobacco is associated with a spirit that edifies the soul. The revelation known as the Word of Wisdom, given to the Prophet Joseph Smith in 1833, speaks against the use of both. It is generally argued that the reason for this prohibition is their detrimental effects on health and on family relationships. In fact, the greater reason is that they restrain the Spirit of the Lord and make it more difficult for us either to receive or to follow the prompting of that Spirit.

Those who were not taught the principles associated with the Word of Wisdom in their mortal probation will have to grow up into these principles before they can obtain a celestial glory.

QUESTION

Why were blacks denied the priesthood for so long?

ANSWER

A meaningful response to this question rests on an understanding of what the priesthood is. That understanding is generally not had by those asking the question. A typical dictionary definition is "the office and vocation of a priest." For a Latter-day Saint, the priesthood is appreciably more than that. The priesthood embraces the power and authority to act in the name of God. It is the authority to represent Deity in teaching the gospel and in performing the ordinances of salvation. Independent of the Spirit of revelation there can be no priesthood. One can hardly profess to speak for a God who will not speak to him. In legal terms, priesthood can be likened to the power of attorney, which is the legal authority by which one person acts in the name of another.

If one accepts the Latter-day Saint claim to priesthood—that is, that only within The Church of Jesus Christ of Latter-day Saints can the authority be found to speak for God—one must at the same time accept what God has said through that priesthood. This was the principle that Christ taught when he told the meridian Twelve, "Ye have not chosen me, but I have chosen you, and ordained you, that ye should go and bring forth fruit, and that your fruit should remain: that whatsoever ye shall ask of the Father in my name, he may give it you" (John 15:16). Thus if one believes that Peter, James, and John did in fact confer the authority they received from the Savior upon Joseph Smith and Oliver Cowdery, one must also believe that the priesthood is to function as those to whom the apostles entrusted it direct. On the other hand, if a person does not believe that Latter-day Saints have this authority, then he cannot be asking the question out of concern for those denied this priesthood. Such a person should be relieved rather than offended that the Latter-day Saints have not given to others a priesthood in which he does not believe.

Answers to questions about why the Lord, in his wisdom, chooses to withhold certain privileges or blessings from certain people for a period of time are generally not known to us. At the time of Moses, the Melchizedek Priesthood was taken from the children of Israel. In its stead they were given the Aaronic, or Lesser, Priesthood. This priesthood was restricted to worthy males of the tribe of Levi. We are told in a revelation on the priesthood that the higher priesthood was taken because the children of Israel failed to sanctify themselves that they might stand in the presence of God (see D&C 84:19–25). This statement, however, leaves unanswered the question about why unborn generations were denied the priesthood because of the failure of their progenitors. Many similar situations exist. Why, for instance, are some nations required to wait so much longer than others to receive the blessings of the gospel? Or why are some couples who want children so badly unable to have them? Or why are some who desire to find a companion to whom they can be sealed in the temple unable to do so?

Our response to such questions must be one of faith. We simply trust the wisdom of God and accept his timetable. We know that he loves all his children and that the withholding of certain blessings for a time and season will not go unrewarded.

QUESTION

Why does a loving God allow so much suffering and sorrow?

ANSWER

We are told, "Adam fell that men might be; and men are, that they might have joy" (2 Nephi 2:25). It is, however, a fallen world into which we are born. All who come into this world will experience death, pain, suffering, and sorrow. Such things are as certain as the rising and setting of the sun. They are the natural effects of the Fall. We were born to experience them. They are part of the curriculum in the school of mortality: in and through and because of them, we learn great lessons. They are both test and schoolmaster. They refine and sanctify. They bring strength and faith, courage and patience, and they give us the opportunity to prove ourselves worthy of a far better world. Without the Fall and its attendant lessons, there would be no need for a Savior or a plan of redemption. Until we have come to the realization of the hopelessness of our mortal condition, we can have no meaningful appreciation of the matchless redemptive work wrought by Christ.

It is true that evil and designing men have added greatly to the suffering and sorrow of this probationary estate. Why this, in addition to all else? we ask. The answer is in the principle of agency. When the power was placed within us to pursue a course that would lead us back to the divine presence, it also empowered us to travel the same distance in the opposite direction. If we have the capacity to become as God is, we must at the same time have the capacity to become as the prince of darkness is. The right of choice must prevail. Lehi stated it succinctly, "For it must needs be, that there is an opposition in all things" (2 Nephi 2:11). We cannot be courageous unless we have been confronted with the opportunity to be courageous. Similarly we cannot be just, merciful, kind, or forgiving without having conquered circumstances which could have evoked an opposite reaction. There can be no righteousness unless there is wickedness; thus all attributes of godliness have their opposite.

When confronted with the effects of this fallen world, we reason rather strangely. In misfortune we often hear people asking, "Why me?" as if God had a quota of evil deeds to dispense and knew full well that we had done less to provoke him than others.

Still ringing in my ears are the words of a person with whom I labored to rectify an injustice. "It was so unfair," that person said. "I was required to suffer for the sins of others." "So was Christ," came the unrestrained response.

All who come into this world do so with the assurance that it will be inequitable and unjust and embrace suffering and sorrow. Mortality is a test and was so intended from the beginning. Seeking fairness in our earthly probation is like searching for stars on a cloudy night; though they are there, we cannot find them. Evil will have its partners and often earn approval and praise while that which is virtuous and good will seemingly be left unnoticed. As to suffering, it seems to find company with the pure and the innocent more often than with those who have provoked its wrath. Of the faithful who are called upon to suffer, the apostle Paul said, "God having provided some better things for them through their sufferings, for without sufferings they could not be made perfect" (JST Hebrews 11:40).

QUESTION

Why do some critics of the Church say that Mormons aren't Christians?

ANSWER

Often those saying that Mormons are not Christians do so with the knowledge that the proper name of the Church is The Church of Jesus Christ of Latter-day Saints. They are equally aware that our faith centers in Christ, as do our doctrines. Most will concede that in practice we are a very Christlike people. Why, then, do they persist in labeling us as a non-Christian cult? The answer is in their history, not in our faith.

The historical Christian world has declared the Bible to be complete and the heavens to be sealed to revelation. They have also declared the biblical descriptions of God to be simply metaphorical and accepted in their place a faith in the incorporeal and incomprehensible God of the early ecumenical councils. Because we do not accept as inspired the conclusions of those councils or embrace the notion that the heavens are sealed to modern revelation and that there are thus no apostles or prophets in our day, we are declared to be both unorthodox and unchristian. The irony is that it is our loyalty to Christian doctrines that gets us the label of non-Christian.

The Catholic and Protestant world declare themselves Christian on the basis of their loyalty to what are known as the Apostolic and Nicene Creeds. Thus the creeds become the issue. To fail to pay allegiance to the creeds is to be branded as non-Christian by those who do pay allegiance to them. These creeds, which represent a departure from biblical Christianity to what even their apologists call "philosophical speculation," define the nature of the Father and the Son in such a way that they are not literally father and son. Indeed, they are no longer viewed as separate and distinct personages, nor are they believed to be corporeal beings. The God of the creeds is "without body, parts, or passions," and the Son is merely the mind or reflection of the Father. Thus for the Latter-day Saints to be accepted as Christian by such a standard, we must deny our faith that Christ is actually and literally the Son of God.

Although we are willing to accord to all people the right to believe "how, where, or what they may" (Article of Faith 11), we are not willing to concede the right to determine whether we are Christian or not. Significantly, the Bible gives no definition of a Christian; rather, those loyal to Christ are called "saints" (Acts 9:13; 26:10). The word *Christian* is found only three times in the biblical text; each time it appears to be an epithet given the Saints by those opposing them (see Acts 11:26; 26:28; 1 Peter 4:16). A dictionary definition of *Christian* is simply one who professes a belief in or follows the teachings of Christ. Because Latter-day Saints both believe in and follow Christ, we declare ourselves to be Christians.

QUESTION

Why are Latter-day Saints so unchristian as to suppose that The Church of Jesus Christ of Latter-day Saints is the only true church?

ANSWER

The essence of Christianity centers on the idea that salvation is in Christ. That being the case, everyone who truly embraces the Christian faith must at the same time embrace the idea that it is only in and through Christ that salvation comes. Christ himself said, "I am the way, the truth, and the life: no man cometh unto the Father, but by me" (John 14:6). Thus the doctrine of all the holy prophets has been that there is "none other name under heaven given among men, whereby we must be saved" (Acts 4:12; see also D&C 18:23; 2 Nephi 25:20; 31:21). Within the ranks of those professing to be Christians there may be differences on the requirements of salvation, but all must agree on the acceptance of Christ as the source of salvation. At issue here is not whether a line must be drawn between the believer and the nonbeliever but simply where that line should be drawn. Latter-day Saints have marked a narrow path; the Protestant world endorses a broad one. For us there is but "one Lord, one faith, one baptism" (Ephesians 4:5) and thus one true Church. For Protestants the point of unity is the saving grace of Christ, beyond which is an immense doctrinal and denominational diversity. They hold it to be unchristian for us to suppose that they are not on the path of salvation while rejecting as outrageous any notion that we could possibly be on that path.

QUESTION

Why is rebaptism necessary in joining the Mormon church?

ANSWER

This question was first asked at the time the Church was organized, back in April 1830. Two separate situations called forth the question. Some individuals had been baptized by the authority restored by John the Baptist in May 1829, and others had been baptized when joining other Christian faiths. That is, some had been baptized by lawful and legal authority, and others had been baptized by those having no authority. Responding to this concern, Joseph Smith inquired of the Lord and received the following: "Behold, I say unto you that all old covenants have I caused to be done away in this thing [the restoration of the gospel]; and this is a new and an everlasting covenant, even that which was from the beginning. Wherefore, although a man should be baptized an hundred times it availeth him nothing, for you cannot enter in at the strait gate by the law of Moses, neither by your dead works. For it is because of your dead works that I have caused this last covenant and this church to be built up unto me, even as in days of old. Wherefore, enter ye in at the gate, as I have commanded, and seek not to counsel your God. Amen" (D&C 22:1–4).

The reference in the revelation to the law of Moses is to the baptisms performed by the authority restored by John the Baptist. As with that ancient law they were adequate for salvation only until a time of fulness—in this instance, for that period between 15 May 1829 when John restored the Aaronic Priesthood and 6 April 1830 when the Church was organized. After the organization of the Church, those who had received this preparatory baptism needed to be baptized into membership in the Church. The reference in the revelation to dead works is to the baptisms performed by those without the authority to do so. As the revelation announces, both situations require a new baptism, for neither had been baptized into membership in the Church.

AT ISSUE

Virtually every objection to the restored gospel reduces itself to the critics' refusal to admit the reality of revelation. To concede the principle of revelation is to concede the victory to Mormonism. Orthodoxy in both Catholicism and Protestantism precludes the possibility that anyone since the ministry of Christ can write scripture. Our message centers on the verity that God can still speak. And if that is the case, then Catholics and Protestants are left to account for the fact that he has not spoken to them and that when he did speak through a living prophet, they refused to listen. We profess no doctrines that do not have modern revelation as their source.

CHAPTER THREE

WHY JOSEPH SMITH?

Why would the Lord choose someone as young and unlearned as Joseph
　　Smith to be his prophet?

What is the difference between a prophet and a seer, and why was it
　　necessary that Joseph Smith be both?

Was Joseph Smith a martyr? Was his death necessary? If so, why?

How can Joseph Smith be referred to in prophecy as both an Israelite and a
　　Gentile?

Was Joseph Smith a Mason? Did Masonry influence the doctrines of the
　　Church?

Was Joseph Smith a gold digger and a seeker of hidden treasures?

Can a prophet err?

Why has there been so much criticism of Joseph Smith among professing
　　Christians?

Why does Mormonism arouse such animosity among so many?

Shouldn't the Church make a greater effort to respond to the ugly,
　　dishonest, foolish, and false things that are said about it?

What are the best evidences that Joseph Smith was a prophet?

WHY DID A WORLD WITH SUCH strongly established Christian traditions, a world that had in its possession the Holy Bible, need a Joseph Smith? Because there was not a man upon the earth who knew God other than by hearsay! Because the kingdom of God cannot be ruled by a book! (God sent Moses, not the Ten Commandments, to lead Israel.) Because the Church organized by the Son of Man was not to be found anywhere upon the earth! Because the doctrines of salvation as taught by Christ and the ancient prophets and apostles had been lost or polluted with the philosophies of men! Because the authority of heaven, the holy priesthood, had been taken from men! Because the covenant or promise made by God to the ancient prophets and his chosen people about their posterity in the last days required fulfillment! Because the time had come to prepare the earth for the return of Christ and his millennial reign!

Long after they had declared the heavens sealed and prophets and apostles to be a thing of the past, the leaders of what called itself the Christian faith met in Nicaea to determine the nature of the God they worshipped. The event is known as the church's first ecumenical council, and out of it came the first formal Christian creed. Everything associated with this council is strangely at odds with the pattern of faith preserved in holy writ. Here prophets were formally replaced by scholars and the revelations of heaven by philosophical speculations. The council was called not by religious leaders but by the Roman emperor Constantine, himself a sun worshipper, who presided over it in regal splendor. His motive lay in the power that he saw within the church to unite his fractured kingdom. The council represented the beginning of an alliance between church and state and the end of religious freedom that would reap untold misery in years to come. Those not acquiescing to the religious decisions of the council were to be banished from their homes by the authority of the state. Indeed, there was nothing in the nature of this council to suggest a purity of purpose.

The council of Nicaea determined that God was incomprehensible and that Jesus of Nazareth, who claimed to be the Son of God, was Logos, meaning that he was the manifestation of the mind of the Father and as such was neither older nor younger than his Father. The new God of Christianity was then denominated as a majestic mystery, both unknown and unknowable. The creed announcing these determinations became the standard by which all doctrine was to be measured. Failure to accept it became a greater bar to acceptance in the traditional Christian world than rejection of the New Testament.

Thus a mist of darkness filled the earth in what we have come to call a universal apostasy. It engulfed the priesthood, its keys, all the ordinances of salvation and the ordinances of blessing, and the offices of the priesthood and its officers. Plain and precious things were taken from holy writ, and other things were added in their place. The purity of every doctrine and principle of salvation was lost. In their stead came an oppressive tyranny over the hearts and minds of men. Where once there had been love unfeigned, now there was a blood-stained sword. Where there had been robes of righteousness, now there were silks, and scarlets, and fine-twined linen, and precious clothing. Worship was replaced by ritual; the prayer of faith, by gold and silver. So darkness covered the earth and gross darkness the minds of the people (see Isaiah 60:2).

In the darkness of the night, the stars of heaven shine forth with greater brilliance. So it was that an unnumbered host of wise and good people reflected such light as they had among those who would look heavenward. In a distant day, brighter lights were to be seen that would chase away the powers of fear, ignorance, and superstition that had ruled for so long. "There was a Calvin, a Zwingli, a Luther, a Wesley; there were wise and good men—morning stars who shone more brightly than their fellows—who arose in every nation. There were men of insight and courage who were sickened by the sins and evils of the night. These great souls hacked and sawed at the chains with which the masses were bound. They sought to do good and to help their fellowmen—all according to the best light and knowledge they had.

"In Germany and France and England and Switzerland and elsewhere groups began to break away from the religion of centuries past. A few rays of light were parting the darkness of the eastern sky.

"Many who sought freedom to worship God according to the dictates of their conscience migrated to America. And in due course, by the power of the Father, a new nation was created, a nation 'conceived in liberty, and dedicated to the proposition that all men were created equal.' (Abraham Lincoln, Gettysburg Address.) The United States of America came into being. Beyond the mountains, now not many leagues away, a new day was gestating in the womb of nature.

"As the earth continued to turn slowly and steadily on its decreed course, as the dawn brightened and the morning light increased, as the Constitution of the United States guaranteed religious freedom, as men were tempered in their feelings and began to view each other with more equity and fairness, as the Bible was published and read by more people, as darkness fled and light increased, the time for the rising of the gospel sun was at hand" (McConkie, in Conference Report, April 1978, 17).

Such was the setting in which the youthful Joseph Smith went into a quiet grove not far from his parents' log home in the spring of 1820 to inquire of the Lord which of all the churches he should join. In response to his humble prayer, both the Father and the Son appeared to him. Calling him by name, the Father said, "This is My Beloved Son. Hear Him!" (Joseph Smith–History 1:17). Everything that Joseph Smith was told and witnessed in the grove that day stood as a rejection of Christian tradition and placed him at odds with it. He learned that the heavens were not sealed and that God could and did speak directly to mankind as he had done in ages past. He learned that both the Father and the Son were personal beings and that they had, contrary to the creeds of

Christendom, body, parts, and passions. He learned that they were separate and distinct and that they were offended by both the creeds and the churches of men.

Though but fourteen years of age when he walked out of the grove that spring morning, Joseph Smith was the most competent witness of God and the truths of heaven on the face of the earth. For the first time in nearly two thousand years someone could speak with authority rather than by way of hearsay. He also had the promise of the Lord that the doctrines of salvation would be restored again in their pristine purity and that the Church and kingdom of God would also be restored to the earth.

Given that there is so little resemblance between modern Christianity and the biblical model after which it claims to be patterned, it is not hard to imagine others coming on the scene claiming to have a divine commission to renew or restore the New Testament order of things. What seems to be universally overlooked is that the great promises of the Lord that still demanded fulfillment were made to the faithful Saints of the Old Testament. What of the promises made to the fathers—Abraham, Issac, and Jacob—relative to their seed? (see Genesis 15:2–6; 17:1–8, 15–19; 22:16–18; 24:60; 26:1–5; 27:46; 28:1–4). These promises centered in the eternal nature of the marriage covenant and the continuation of the family unit throughout the eternities. The restoration of the Abrahamic covenant stands at the heart of this great dispensation in which all promises of the Lord must find fulfillment. The length and breadth of the labor of which we speak creates the demand for more than a prophet. It requires a seer, one who can see both past and present, to envision all that is involved. Needed here is one who can restore the testimony of the ancients and bring us the knowledge of the promises made to our faithful fathers in ages past. Only then can a system be established whereby we as their posterity can be gathered to the truths of salvation known to them and, as necessary, be restored to the lands of promise. But this is not all, for salvation is a family affair and requires the sealing, or binding, of families together from the beginning of time to the end thereof. This in turn requires the teaching of the gospel to those in the world of spirits and the performance of the ordinances of salvation for and in their behalf. No would-be prophet has pretended to such a vision except the sorrowful and unimaginative souls who have stolen every thought they ever had from the Prophet Joseph Smith.

Such events required the leadership of one who could be trained by the Lord even from his youth, one who stood entirely independent of the doctrines and philosophies of the world, one whose testimony could be believed by all who were honest in heart. Such was the role that Joseph Smith was destined to play. Thus the Prophet was able to characterize himself in these words: "I am like a huge, rough stone rolling down from a high mountain; and the only polishing I get is when some corner gets rubbed off by coming in contact with something else, striking with accelerated force against religious bigotry, priestcraft, lawyer-craft, doctor-craft, lying editors, suborned judges and jurors, and the authority of perjured executives, backed by mobs, blasphemers, licentious and corrupt men and women—all hell knocking off a corner here and a corner there. Thus I will become a smooth and polished shaft in the quiver of the Almighty, who will give me dominion over all and every one of them, when their refuge of lies shall fail, and their hiding place shall be destroyed, while these smooth-polished stones with which I come in contact become marred" (*Teachings of the Prophet Joseph Smith*, 304).

QUESTION

Why would the Lord choose someone as young and unlearned as Joseph Smith to be his prophet?

ANSWER

Joseph Smith was fourteen years of age when the Father and the Son appeared to him in the Sacred Grove, seventeen when

Moroni first appeared to him, and twenty-four when he organized the Church. His formal education consisted of a few seasons in a one-room schoolhouse. Well might we ask, Why would the Lord choose someone with so little training for such a monumental task? As a prophet he would be called upon to translate the Book of Mormon, the Bible—both Old and New Testaments—and the Abraham papyrus. Further, he would be called upon to articulate the whole message of the Restoration, including a host of revelations, which of necessity must stand the test of time and the scrutiny of the world's finest scholars and of countless critics. He would be called upon to write more scripture than the dozen most prolific writers of the Bible combined, doing so under the most trying and difficult of circumstances while uniting people of every nation, kindred, and tongue into one faith. Given the nature of the task, would it not have been more appropriate for the Lord to call as his prophet one of the great and learned men of the world? Would not his so doing give more credibility to the message of Mormonism?

Strangely, we declare that Joseph Smith's lack of learning—by the standards of the world, that is—was a preeminent qualification. We say this because his labor was not of the world. There was to be no confusion about the fact that he was an instrument of the Lord and that the labors he performed could not have been his own. "The best way to obtain truth and wisdom is not to ask it from books, but to go to God in prayer, and obtain divine teaching," he said (*Teachings of the Prophet Joseph Smith*, 191). He also said, "Could you gaze into heaven five minutes, you would know more than you would by reading all that ever was written on the subject" (ibid., 324).

Academic training, or the learning of men, was of little moment in the labor to which Joseph Smith was called. "I call upon the weak things of the world," the Lord has said, "those who are unlearned and despised, to thrash the nations by the power of my Spirit; and their arm shall be my arm, and I will be their shield and their buckler; and I will gird up their loins, and they shall fight manfully for me; and their enemies shall be under their feet; and I will let fall the sword in their behalf, and by the fire of mine indignation will I preserve them" (D&C 35:13–14).

The translation of the Book of Mormon was accomplished "by the gift and power of God," not by the learning of men (D&C 135:3; see also 20:8). The same is true of all the Prophet's labors as both translator and revelator, for it is the prophet who is the instrument of the Lord, not the Lord who is the instrument of the prophet. Even the Savior himself said, "My Father is greater than I" (John 14:28). Any servant of the Lord who sets at "naught the counsels of God, and follows after the dictates of his own will and carnal desires" will "fall and incur the vengeance of a just God upon him" (D&C 3:4).

The calling of an unlearned prophet, as Isaiah described him, dramatizes that the work is not man's but the Lord's and that there is no salvation in the precepts of men (see Isaiah 29:12–13). "The weak things of the world shall come forth and break down the mighty and strong ones," the Lord has declared, "that man should not counsel his fellow man, neither trust in the arm of flesh" (D&C 1:19). Indeed, "cursed is he that putteth his trust in man, or maketh flesh his arm, or shall hearken unto the precepts of men, save their precepts shall be given by the power of the Holy Ghost" (2 Nephi 28:31).

The heart and mind of Joseph Smith were virgin soil. Nothing needed to be uprooted before the seeds of the restored gospel could be planted there, nor could it be supposed that the youthful Joseph was the creator of those seeds.

QUESTION

What is the difference between a prophet and a seer, and why was it necessary that Joseph Smith be both?

ANSWER

A prophet is a man who has the Spirit of prophecy, meaning the testimony of Jesus (see Revelation 19:10). Those holding the office of a prophet have the authority to speak for God. The prophet standing at the head of the Church is the covenant spokesman for the Lord. None have done better in describing the prophetic office than President Anthony W. Ivins, who explained that "a careful study of the etymology of the word and of the lives, works and character of the prophets of old makes clear the fact that a prophet was, and is, one called to act as God's messenger. He is to teach men the character of God, and define and make known to the people, his will. He is to denounce sin, and declare the punishment of transgression. He is to be above all else a preacher of righteousness, and when the people depart from the path which he has marked out for them to follow, is to call them back to the true faith. He is an interpreter of the scripture, and declares its meaning and application. When future events are to be declared he predicts them, but his direct, and most important calling is to be a forth-teller, or director of present policy, rather than a foreteller of that which is to come" (in Conference Report, October 1925, 20).

As marvelous as the office of a prophet is, we are told that "a seer is greater than a prophet" (Mosiah 8:15, 17). With this office rests the ability to see both the past and the future. The great seers have been entrusted with seeric devices (seerstones or the Urim and Thummim) to aid both in receiving revelation and in translating scriptural records from unknown tongues (see Mosiah 28:13–14). The restoration of all things that was to take place in our dispensation required a seer to restore it and a prophet to declare it.

Joseph Smith was prophetically described by his progenitor, Joseph of Egypt, as "a choice seer" (2 Nephi 3:6–7). Through him we are invited to see both past and future. Through him we learn of our premortal estate and of the Grand Council in Heaven. We learn that Adam was Michael, who led the army of the Lord in the great war in heaven, and that he holds the "keys of salvation" and the "keys of the universe" (D&C 78:16; Smith, *Teachings of the Prophet Joseph Smith,* 157). Through him we gain an expanded view of the Creation and the true nature of the fall of Adam. Through him we gain knowledge and insight into the major dispensations of the past. We learn that the faithful of ages past had a testimony of Christ, that they knew of the doctrines of salvation, and that they participated in the ordinances of salvation. From the records restored by Joseph Smith, we learn of their testimony and of the doctrines of salvation, and through the visions and revelations granted them we receive counsel and warnings directed to our day.

QUESTION

Was Joseph Smith a martyr? Was his death necessary? If so, why?

ANSWER

The word *martyr* comes from a Greek word meaning "witness." It is generally held to mean one who voluntarily submits to death for the Christian faith, but in a broader sense it is used to describe one who has experienced great suffering or death on account of loyalty to the gospel. Critics of the Church like to argue that Joseph Smith was not a martyr because he made an effort to defend himself when he was killed. The purpose of the argument is to avoid giving credence, honor, or respect to the Prophet, who willingly submitted himself to arrest on false charges and went to Carthage knowing he would die there (see D&C 135:4). The idea that a true martyr cannot resist an attempt to take his or her life grows out of the false zeal associated with the early Christian era. Many of the so-called martyrs of that day sought death. Their efforts grew out of the apostate notion that the body was to be eschewed, that it was a prison in which the spirit had been confined by the fall of Adam, and that to rid themselves of it was a matchless good. Latter-day Saints reject such theological travesty while granting the title of martyr to those who have experienced great suffering and dangers associated with being true to the faith and who have eventually lost their lives in that cause.

As to the necessity of the Prophet's death, the Lord said, "I took him to myself." By way of explanation he added, "Many have marveled because of his death; but it was needful that he should seal his testimony with his blood, that he might be honored and the wicked might be condemned" (D&C 136:38–39). Of the deaths of Joseph and Hyrum Smith the scripture declares: "The testators are now dead, and their testament is in force. . . .

"They were innocent of any crime, as they had often been proved before, and were only confined in jail by the conspiracy of traitors and wicked men; and their *innocent blood* on the floor of Carthage jail is a broad seal affixed to 'Mormonism' that cannot be rejected by any court on earth, and their *innocent blood* on the escutcheon of the State of Illinois, with the broken faith of the State as pledged by the governor, is a witness to the truth of the everlasting gospel that all the world cannot impeach; and their *innocent blood* on the banner of liberty, and on the *magna charta* of the United States, is an ambassador for the religion of Jesus Christ, that will touch the hearts of honest men among all nations; and their *innocent blood*, with the innocent blood of all the martyrs under the altar that John saw, will cry unto the Lord of Hosts till he avenges that blood on the earth. Amen" (D&C 135:5–7).

QUESTION

How can Joseph Smith be referred to in prophecy as both an Israelite and a Gentile?

ANSWER

In a revelation given as early as August 1831, Joseph Smith was told that he was a descendant of Abraham (see D&C 132:30). He was also told that he was a lawful heir, "according to the flesh," to the priesthood, which was promised to the descendants of Abraham (see D&C 86:9–10; Abraham 2:9, 11). Prophecy further identified him as a direct lineal descendant of Joseph of Egypt (see JST Genesis 50:27, 33; 2 Nephi 3:7, 15). More particularly, he is represented as being a descendant of Ephraim and as having some of the blood of Jesse (see D&C 113:4). Notwithstanding this, the title page to the Book of Mormon, which was written by Moroni, says that it will come forth by the hand of a Gentile. Reference here is to his citizenship in a Gentile nation, thus fulfilling prophecies which also declare that the gospel will grow forth from a mighty Gentile nation and that those who carry it will also be Gentiles (see 1 Nephi 15:13; 22:7–12; Mormon 5:15). Thus Joseph Smith was a literal descendant of the house of Israel while at the same time being a citizen of a Gentile nation. He was an Israelite by descent and a Gentile by culture.

QUESTION

Was Joseph Smith a Mason? Did Masonry influence the doctrines of the Church?

ANSWER

Joseph Smith and many of the leading brethren of that day were Masons. The question implies that there is something secret or sinister in their Masonic affiliation. This was hardly the case. The Saints who built Nauvoo built a Masonic lodge there. It is among the buildings that have been restored in Nauvoo, and visitors are encouraged to visit it. About fifteen hundred Latter-day Saint men entered the Masonic order during the Nauvoo period; others had joined earlier in the Kirtland era. Anti-Mormon critics have attempted to argue that Joseph Smith copied the Masonic ritual in the temple endowment. It is not inconceivable that the Prophet, sensing something about the ancient roots of Masonry, inquired of the Lord about it. In that sense it may have been one of the influences that prepared the way for the revelations that restored the ceremonies of the temple. If the Prophet was trying to copy Masonry, he certainly chose the wrong time, the wrong place, and the wrong people to do it with. Many of the leaders of the Church were involved in the Masonic lodge in Nauvoo, among them those with whom he worked most closely and who were destined to be his successors in leading the Church. These were men who would yet prove their willingness to sacrifice their all to build temples and see that every faithful Latter-day Saint had the privilege of participating in the ordinances of the temple.

The idea that the kind of faith and courage common to our pioneer forebears grew out of rituals copied from a fraternal organization is ludicrous. The experiences the Latter-day Saints have had in the temple have come too often and are too real for anyone to suppose that they stem from a borrowed ceremony. Similarly, the assurance that we will be endowed with power from on high does not lack for proof among our people.

QUESTION

Was Joseph Smith a gold digger and a seeker of hidden treasures?

ANSWER

"One of the first objections that was urged against Joseph Smith," recalled President Brigham Young in 1868, "was that he was a money digger; and now," he said, "the digging of gold is considered an honorable and praiseworthy employment. They are hunting for gold all over the country, doing the very thing which they condemned in him. The next fault they found with Joseph and the Saints was that they were stirring up the slaves to rebellion against their masters; and this was published abroad. Have they not done, and are they not now doing, the very thing for which they falsely blamed the Saints?" (in *Journal of Discourses*, 12:165). Addressing the same issue, Elder Wilford Woodruff observed: "They formerly found a great deal of fault with Joseph Smith, because they said he was a gold digger; but since then nearly all the Christian world have turned gold diggers. Hundreds of thousands of them have run into this western country to dig gold; and, while they formerly found fault with us for digging gold they have latterly found fault because we do not dig it" (in *Journal of Discourses*, 14:36).

Joseph Smith explained the origin of the stories about his being a gold digger: "In the year 1823 my father's family met with a great affliction by the death of my eldest brother, Alvin. In the month of October, 1825, I hired with an old gentleman by the name of Josiah Stoal, who lived in Chenango county, State of New York. He had heard something of a silver mine having been opened by the Spaniards in Harmony, Susquehanna county, State of Pennsylvania; and had, previous to my hiring to him, been digging, in order, if possible, to discover the mine. After I went to live with him, he took me, with the rest of his hands, to dig for the silver mine, at which I continued to work for nearly a month, without success in our undertaking, and finally I prevailed with the old gentleman to cease digging after it. Hence arose the very prevalent story of my having been a money-digger" (Joseph Smith–History 1:56).

QUESTION

Can a prophet err?

ANSWER

Mormonism does not embrace the notion of the infallibility for any man, save Jesus only, nor does it embrace the idea of the infallibility of scriptural records. Of Elijah the scriptures attest that he was "a man subject to like passions as we are," even though he had the power to seal the heavens to rain and then bring it forth again at his command (James 5:17–18). Teaching the same principle, Moroni said, "Condemn me not because of mine imperfection, neither my father, because of his imperfection, neither them who have written before him; but rather give thanks unto God that he hath made manifest unto you our imperfections, that ye may learn to be more wise than we have been" (Mormon 9:31). Of the restored gospel the Lord said, "These commandments are of me, and were given unto my servants in their weakness, after the manner of their language, that they might come to understanding. And inasmuch as they erred it might be made known; and inasmuch as they sought wisdom they might be instructed; and inasmuch as they sinned they might be chastened, that they might repent; and inasmuch as they were humble they might be made strong, and blessed from on high, and receive knowledge from time to time" (D&C 1:24–28).

It will be recalled that Joseph Smith was severely disciplined by the Lord for the loss of the 116 manuscript pages of the Book of Mormon. Because of the Prophet's disobedience, the Lord withdrew his Spirit from Joseph Smith and allowed him to walk in darkness (see D&C 10:2; 19:20). Speaking of those events the Lord said, "How oft you have transgressed the commandments and the laws of God, and have gone on in the persuasions of men. . . . You should have been faithful; and he would have extended his arm and supported you against all the fiery darts of the adversary, and he would have been with you in every time of trouble" (D&C 3:6–8). Nor was this the only occasion on which the Prophet was chastened by the Lord. In a revelation received some five years later we read these words: "I say unto Joseph Smith, Jun.—You have not kept the commandments, and must needs stand rebuked before the Lord; your family must needs repent and forsake some things, and give more earnest heed unto your sayings, or be removed out of their place" (D&C 93:47–48).

It would be foolish to suppose that there is some point, office, or position at which one can arrive in this mortal probation that places one above temptation or beyond the reach of mistakes common to mortal men. Speaking to the newly called apostles in the New World, the resurrected Lord said, "Verily, verily, I say unto you, ye must watch and pray always, lest ye be tempted by the devil, and ye be led away captive by him" (3 Nephi 18:15). To Peter, who was destined to stand at the head of the meridian Church, the Lord said, "Simon, Simon, behold, Satan hath desired to have you, that he may sift you as wheat" (Luke 22:31). Again, to the first Quorum of the Twelve of our day, the Lord directed Thomas B. Marsh, their president, to pray for them and to "admonish them sharply for my name's sake, and let them be admonished for all their sins, and be ye faithful before me unto my name"—this with the promise that "after their temptations, and much tribulation, behold, I, the Lord, will feel after them, and if they harden not their hearts, and stiffen not their necks against me, they shall be converted, and I will heal them" (D&C 112:12–13).

Well might we say that the best of temptations are reserved for the best of men. There is no immunity to the frailties of the flesh in offices or position. All must work out their own salvation with fear and trembling (see Philippians 2:12). Thus we make no claim that our prophets are infallible in behavior or in doctrine. We do claim, however, that they are among the best men living on the earth and that they teach the best doctrine the world has ever heard.

QUESTION

Why has there been so much criticism of Joseph Smith among professing Christians?

ANSWER

Shortly after he received what we have come to call his first vision, Joseph Smith learned that sharing his experience "excited a great deal of prejudice" against him by "professors of religion." This notwithstanding the fact that he was, as he described himself, "an obscure boy, only between fourteen and fifteen years of age," whose circumstances in life were "such as to make a boy of no consequence in the world, yet men of high standing would take notice sufficient to excite the public mind against" him to foster a spirit of bitter persecution. This, he said, "was common among all the sects—all united to persecute me. It caused me serious reflection then, and often has since, how very strange it was that an obscure boy, of a little over fourteen years of age, and one, too, who was doomed to the necessity of obtaining a scanty maintenance by his daily labor, should be thought a character of sufficient importance to attract the attention of the great ones of the most popular sects of the day, and in a manner to create in them a spirit of the most bitter persecution and reviling" (Joseph Smith–History 1:22–23).

If the youthful Joseph Smith was as deluded as his critics felt he was, it was their Christian duty to reach out to him in love. In patience and kindness they should have attempted to correct his errant ways. Instead they treated him with bitterness and contempt. From this we can only conclude that the adversary of truth knows his enemies even from their youth. From that day to this, the criticism of Joseph Smith has not ceased, nor would we expect it to. The greater the truth, the greater the heresy that opposes it. No man in earth's history has been responsible for restoring more truth than has the Prophet Joseph Smith, and thus we can suppose that no man in earth's history will have more evil spoken of him. When Joseph was only seventeen years of age, Moroni told him that his name would be had for both good and evil among those of every nation, kindred, and tongue (see Joseph Smith–History 1:33). "The workers of iniquity will seek your overthrow: they will circulate falsehoods to destroy your reputation, and also will seek to take your life," Moroni told Joseph. Notwithstanding this, the Prophet was promised that the great work restored by him would "increase the more [it is] opposed" (*Messenger and Advocate* 2 [October 1835]: 199).

It is the practice among people of evil disposition that when they can't refute a person's doctrine, they attack the person's character. Such has been the lot of righteous individuals in all ages. "Blessed are they which are persecuted for righteousness' sake," the Savior said, "for theirs is the kingdom of heaven. Blessed are ye, when men shall revile you, and persecute you, and shall say all manner of evil against you falsely, for my sake. Rejoice, and be exceeding glad: for great is your reward in heaven: for so persecuted they the prophets which were before you" (Matthew 5:10–12).

QUESTION

Why does Mormonism arouse such animosity among so many?

ANSWER

Although the religions of men are often tolerant of each other, they cannot abide the presence of living prophets and the truths of salvation. Their bitterness and opposition toward Mormonism are an essential witness of its truthfulness. Validity draws the fire. If Mormonism is true, then those of all other faiths are in need of repentance and baptism; they must conform to the teachings of living prophets, and they must dissociate themselves from things that are of the world. We would not suppose that such a message could go unopposed. If our message does not give offense to that which is ungodly, it has no claim on that which is heavenly. It has been properly said that light and darkness will never meet and that Christ and Satan will never shake hands.

If Mormonism were not true, it could be ignored. The fact that Satan and his cohorts cannot leave it alone is an evidence of its truthfulness. There is no neutrality where the truths of salvation are concerned. A man by the name of Behunnin once told the Prophet Joseph Smith that if he were ever to leave the Church, he would not do as others had done and turn and fight against it. "I would," he said, "go to some remote place where Mormonism had never been heard of, settle down, and no one would ever learn that I knew anything about it." Joseph Smith's response was immediate: "Brother Behunnin, you don't know what you would do. [Then, referring to apostates who were fighting against the Church, he said:] No doubt these men once thought as you do. Before you joined this Church you stood on neutral ground. When the gospel was preached good and evil were set before you. You could choose either or neither. There were two opposite masters inviting you to serve them. When you joined this Church you enlisted to serve God. When you did that you left the neutral ground, and you never can get back on to it. Should you forsake the Master you enlisted to serve it will be by the instigation of the evil one, and you will follow his dictation and be his servant" (*Juvenile Instructor* 27 [15 August 1892]: 492).

The creeds of Christendom describe God as an incomprehensible mystery while declaring that revelation has ceased. Mormonism, on the other hand, declares that the heavens are open and that both God and the truths of salvation can be known with perfect surety. There is no common ground here, which is obvious to them, if not to us.

QUESTION

Shouldn't the Church make a greater effort to respond to the ugly, dishonest, foolish, and false things that are said about it?

ANSWER

Little is to be gained by kicking skunks or entering into a spitting contest with camels. We accomplish more in the declaration of the truth—that is, in teaching the message the Lord has given us—than in responding to the endless falsehoods that are hurled against us. Few falsehoods deserve response. The adversary will often use such things to divert our attention from the greater labor of declaring our message.

President Ezra Taft Benson shared an experience he had as a young missionary in the British Isles that illustrates the principle. He and his companion were invited to speak in the South Shields Branch. They were asked to respond to the "lies that were being printed about the Church" for the benefit of the investigators who would be present. Elder Benson was assigned to speak on the Apostasy and prepared himself to do so. When he stood to speak, he felt a strong impression to talk about the Book of Mormon, which he did. Afterwards, he said, he couldn't recall what he had said, though he had enjoyed a great freedom of expression. At the conclusion of the meeting, he was surrounded by nonmembers who told him that while he was speaking, they had received a witness that Joseph Smith was a prophet and they were now ready for baptism (see Dew, *Ezra Taft Benson*, 55). Our commission is to bear witness of the restored gospel among every nation, kindred, tongue, and people, not to respond to every objection the adversary and his legions raise against it.

QUESTION

What are the best evidences that Joseph Smith was a prophet?

ANSWER

The greatest evidences that Joseph Smith was a prophet are found in the doctrines he restored. He was first and foremost a witness of Christ. Joseph Smith was the great revelator of Christ and the doctrines of salvation for our dispensation. As such he taught more truth about the Son of God than any other gospel teacher or writer of whom we have record. The First Vision is by itself sufficient evidence of his prophetic calling. For nearly two thousand years mankind's knowledge of God was confined to hearsay, tradition, and speculation. When Joseph Smith walked out of the Sacred Grove, he had talked to God face to face. Though but fourteen years of age he was the most competent witness of Deity upon the earth. He knew that the heavens were not sealed, that God was not speechless. He knew that God was a personal being in the likeness of man, as was his Beloved Son. He knew also that no church on the face of the earth possessed either the doctrines of salvation or the authority to speak on behalf of the heavens.

Through revelations given to Joseph Smith, we learn a host of truths lost to the rest of the Bible-believing world. We learn that we are all the offspring of God and thus possess the capacity to become as he is. We learn that the resurrection is the inseparable union of body and spirit and that as corporeal beings it is intended that we come forth from the grave with gender to continue our roles as fathers and mothers and husbands and wives. We learn that for those sealed by the power of the priesthood the family unit is eternal. Associated with this doctrine that binds the family from generation to generation, we learn that the principles of the gospel are taught in the world of spirits and, in an illustration of the goodness of God, we learn of the gradation of glories that are associated with the resurrection and the judgment by works.

The Book of Mormon is a powerful evidence of the prophetic office of Joseph Smith. It is intended to be taken to people of every kindred, tongue, and nation. No honest truth-seeker can study its doctrines and fail to conclude that Joseph Smith is indeed a prophet of God. The same is true of the Doctrine and Covenants, the Pearl of Great Price, and the Joseph Smith Translation. In countless ways they evidence that the truths being restored reach well beyond the wisdom of the mortal mind.

AT ISSUE

To acknowledge that Joseph Smith was a prophet is to acknowledge the verity of the revelations that he received. It is to concede that the traditional Christian world is without the authority to speak for God and that the truths of salvation are found only within The Church of Jesus Christ of Latter-day Saints. Within those revelations is more evidence of the divine calling of Joseph Smith than exists for any other prophet who ever lived. Of the gospel restored by Joseph Smith the Lord said, "I have sent mine everlasting covenant into the world, to be a light to the world, and to be a standard for my people, and for the Gentiles to seek to it, and to be a messenger before my face to prepare the way before me" (D&C 45:9).

The message evidences its own truthfulness. Unable to refute the doctrine, those who oppose it are most often found attacking the character of the Prophet. So it was that Moroni told the youthful Joseph Smith that his name would be had "for good and evil among all nations, kindred, and tongues, or that it should be both good and evil spoken of among all people" (Joseph Smith–History 1:33). Affirming the same prophecy, the Lord told Joseph Smith that the ends of the earth would inquire after his name, that fools would hold him in derision, and that hell would rage against him. Nevertheless, the Lord said, "The pure in heart, and the wise, and the noble, and the virtuous, shall seek counsel, and authority, and blessings constantly from under thy hand" (D&C 122:1–2).

CHAPTER FOUR

GRACE AND MERCY

How does the Latter-day Saint doctrine of salvation by grace differ from
   the doctrine of grace as taught in the evangelical world?
What does it mean to say that we were born under the covenant? What
   difference does it make?
Can those who are converts to the Church and thus were not born under
   the covenant receive the same blessings as those who were?
What is believing blood?
Do those who have entered into the new and everlasting covenant of
   marriage have the promise that they will not lose any of their children?
Will all those who die before arriving at the age of accountability be saved
   in the highest degree of the celestial kingdom, or will they have to be
   tested? Do they have to receive temple ordinances?
How many of our Father's children will inherit the celestial kingdom?

DURING MY GROWING-UP YEARS in the Church, I cannot
remember a single Sunday School, priesthood, or seminary
lesson on the subject of grace. Nor do I remember anyone speaking
on the matter in sacrament meeting. Grace was generally thought

to be a Protestant doctrine, and Latter-day Saints knew that all blessings were predicated upon obedience to gospel laws. I went into the mission field, as I think most of the young men and women of my generation did, thinking that all I needed to know on the subject was that when Paul taught grace, he was speaking to Jews who didn't understand that they could no longer be saved by the works of the law of Moses. I could also quote, but had little meaningful understanding of, the third Article of Faith, which states: "We believe that through the Atonement of Christ, all mankind may be saved, by obedience to the laws and ordinances of the Gospel." What is most embarrassing about all this is that I was completely ignorant that the doctrine of Christ's grace is one of the great themes of the Book of Mormon—the book and message that I as a missionary had been commissioned to declare.

More recent years have witnessed a growing interest in and enthusiasm for the doctrine. Books are being written on it, and no New Testament symposium is complete without someone sharing some new insight on the teachings of Paul. What still seems to be missing is the realization that if the message of the Restoration embraces the doctrine of grace, then it will be taught in the scriptures of the Restoration with a plainness and clarity that far exceeds that of Paul or the New Testament. By its very definition, a gospel dispensation is a period of time in which the doctrines of salvation are dispensed anew from the heavens in such a manner that they are free from the misconceptions in which the long night of apostate darkness may have clothed them.

That is precisely what has happened. The Book of Mormon, which lays the theological foundations of Mormonism, is the source book on the subject of grace. In contrast to the Bible, in which we are almost entirely dependent on the writings of Paul for an understanding of this doctrine, in the Book of Mormon we have Lehi, his sons Nephi and Jacob, King Benjamin, Abinadi, and the great teaching duo of Alma and Amulek—all delivering great discourses on grace. Martin Luther would have loved the

Book of Mormon, as does any honest disciple of the doctrine of grace who reads it with an open mind under the tutelage of the Holy Ghost. To suppose that we, like the Protestant world, are solely dependent on the teachings of Paul for our understanding of the doctrine of grace is to miss the whole point of the Restoration. In fact, it is because there was a restoration of the gospel that we have a meaningful understanding of what Paul was teaching.

Let us then turn to the Book of Mormon—our new witness for Christ—to clearly establish what is involved in the doctrine known to us as salvation by grace. Lehi, the book's first prophet, sets the course for us as he instructs his son Jacob. "I know that thou art redeemed," Lehi told his son, and note the reason, "because of the righteousness of thy Redeemer" (2 Nephi 2:3). If the Book of Mormon were a forgery, we might have expected this passage to read: "I know that thou art redeemed because of your righteousness and obedience in keeping the laws and ordinances of the gospel." But father Lehi taught no such thing. Redemption does not come from our righteousness; it comes from the merit and mercy of Christ. Lehi continued: "The law is given unto men. And by the law no flesh is justified; or, by the law men are cut off." Now at this point we could argue as we do with Paul's teachings and say, Well, it is the law of Moses that he is talking about, but Lehi does not leave us that option. Completing his thought, he said, "Yea, by the temporal law they were cut off; and also, by the spiritual law they perish from that which is good, and become miserable forever" (2 Nephi 2:5).

What Lehi says is that our obedience to the laws and ordinances of the gospel will not save us. Law is not our Savior. God ordained the laws; the laws did not ordain God. Yet even if we were foolish enough to suppose that the power of salvation was to be found in the laws, we still couldn't be saved because none of us could be justified by the law. That is, the law could not acquit us; it could not find us innocent because we have all sinned and fallen short of the demands of the law. Lehi said further: "Wherefore, redemption cometh in and through the Holy Messiah; for he is full of grace and truth. Behold, he offereth himself a sacrifice for sin, to answer the ends of the law,"—now note this plain and precious declaration—"unto all those who have a broken heart and a contrite spirit; and unto none else can the ends of the law be answered" (2 Nephi 2:6–7).

The doctrine is perfect. It needs no tailoring to fit comfortably alongside the necessity of individual responsibility. There is no cheap grace here. On the one hand, no one will be justified by the law. We are all imperfect and thus tainted by the effects of sin. Our righteousness will not save us. We are all dependent on the mercy of Christ, on his merit, his grace. Nevertheless, the fulness of that mercy, merit, and grace is extended to those "who have a broken heart and a contrite spirit and unto none else" (2 Nephi 2:7). In inspired words penned by Joseph Smith, we are told that Christ rose from the dead "that he might bring all men unto him, on conditions of repentance" (D&C 18:12). "Thus," Amulek said, "he shall bring salvation to all those who shall believe on his name; this being the intent of this last sacrifice, to bring about the bowels of mercy, which overpowereth justice, and bringeth about means unto men that they may have faith unto repentance. And thus mercy can satisfy the demands of justice, and encircles them in the arms of safety, while he that exercises no faith unto repentance is exposed to the whole law of the demands of justice; therefore only unto him that has faith unto repentance is brought about the great and eternal plan of redemption" (Alma 34:15–16).

Redemption comes only on Christ's terms, and his terms are "a broken heart and a contrite spirit" (2 Nephi 2:7). That spirit is to manifest itself in a covenant relationship. Thus, the principles of faith, repentance, and baptism become companions to the doctrine of grace. "How great the importance," Lehi said, "to make these things known unto the inhabitants of the earth, that they may know that there is no flesh that can dwell in the presence of God, save it be through the merits, and mercy, and grace of the

Holy Messiah, who layeth down his life according to the flesh, and taketh it again by the power of the Spirit, that he may bring to pass the resurrection of the dead, being the first that should rise. Wherefore, he is the firstfruits unto God, inasmuch as he shall make intercession for all the children of men; and they that believe in him shall be saved" (2 Nephi 2:8–9).

In a marvelously instructive discourse on the subject of baptism, Nephi tells us that this sacred ordinance constitutes the gate through which we must enter to begin our journey on the strait and narrow path that leads to eternal life. In response to the question, Is all done when we enter in through the gate? he answered, "Behold, I say unto you, Nay; for ye have not come thus far save it were by the word of Christ with unshaken faith in him, relying wholly upon the merits of him who is mighty to save." Thus, he explained, we are required to "press forward with a steadfastness in Christ, having a perfect brightness of hope, and a love of God and of all men. Wherefore, if ye shall press forward, feasting upon the word of Christ, and endure to the end, behold, thus saith the Father: Ye shall have eternal life. And now, behold, my beloved brethren, this is the way; and there is none other way nor name given under heaven whereby man can be saved in the kingdom of God" (2 Nephi 31:19–21).

Again the doctrine is perfect. It is by the grace of the Father that there is a path that leads to eternal life. And it is by the grace of the Son that through the waters of baptism we are able to take upon ourselves his name, meaning his attributes and powers, and so can place ourselves upon that path. Then if we "press forward with a steadfastness in Christ" (2 Nephi 31:20), feasting upon his word, and enduring to the end, we have the promise that we will hear the voice of the Father saying, "Ye shall have eternal life" (2 Nephi 31:20)—that is, we shall be saved.

Though he had charity for all men, Nephi said, "For none of these can I hope except they shall be reconciled unto Christ, and enter into the narrow gate, and walk in the strait path which leads

to life, and continue in the path until the end of the day of probation" (2 Nephi 33:9). Our reconciliation with Christ requires obedience to the laws and ordinances of the gospel. It cannot be
reduced to an expression of belief alone, for the command is that
we follow him, and that implies action (see 2 Nephi 31:10–16).

QUESTION

How does the Latter-day Saint doctrine of salvation by grace
differ from the doctrine of grace as taught in the evangelical world?

ANSWER

Through the scriptures of the Restoration, we as Latter-day
Saints have been given a wealth of understanding not yet known
to those not of our faith. For instance, in seeking to understand the
doctrine of grace, we understand that God does not do for us what
we can do for ourselves. That understanding is simply a manifestation of the verity that we were created in the image and likeness
of God. Body, mind, and spirit were all given us by a divine
Creator, and thus it is expected that they be used for both divine
and eternal purposes. We are expected to do all the wholesome
and good things that are within our capacity to do. To suppose that
we have the capacity to labor in our own behalf, to advance "from
grace to grace" (D&C 93:13), and then to suppose that the atoning sacrifice of Christ excuses us from the responsibility to do so is
to argue that the purpose of the gospel is to excuse us from being
godlike.

Indeed, the gospel of Jesus Christ comes to us in the form of a
covenant. "My blood," Christ said, "shall not cleanse them if they
hear me not" (D&C 29:17). The promise is that he will bring "all
men unto him, on conditions of repentance" (D&C 18:12;
138:19). Teaching this principle, King Benjamin explained that
through the Atonement, salvation would come "to him that
should put his trust in the Lord, and should be diligent in keeping

his commandments, and continue in the faith even unto the end of his life" (Mosiah 4:6). Similarly, Alma explained that "only unto him that has faith unto repentance is brought about the great and eternal plan of redemption" (Alma 34:16).

The priesthood could be cited as a second illustration. The gospel embraces ordinances of salvation, which must be performed by legal administrators, meaning those who hold the appropriate priesthood and act under the direction of those called to preside over it. For instance, baptism is called the gate to the kingdom of heaven (see 2 Nephi 31:17; D&C 43:7). If we do not enter in through the gate, we cannot obtain entrance. In like manner, we are told that without eternal marriage, we cannot enter into the highest degree within the celestial kingdom (see D&C 131:1–4). The revelations also tell us that the higher, or holy, priesthood "administereth the gospel" (D&C 84:19). So it is that the ordinances of salvation—baptism and eternal marriage being our illustrations—are necessary on our part. The grace of Christ does not excuse us from entering into these sacred covenants and from the necessity of living up to the covenants we have made.

There are also many other ways in which the Latter-day Saint perception of the doctrine of salvation by grace vastly exceeds that of the sectarian world. When we address God as our "Father in Heaven," we do so because we understand him to be exactly that. Life did not begin with our birth into mortality, nor were we created out of nothing. We are the spirit offspring of eternal parents. We were born in a premortal estate, as was our elder brother, Christ. He was known to us then as he is now, as the Firstborn, meaning the firstborn of all the Father's spirit children. It was by the grace of the Father that we were born into that spirit realm. In and through his grace, laws were ordained whereby we might become like him. That required the creation of this earth so that we might be born into a physical world where we might obtain a physical body, like our heavenly parents', and where we might prove our willingness to be obedient to God's commandments.

Thus when we speak of the grace of God, we speak both of the grace of the Father and of the grace of the Son, for it was by the grace of the Father that we were created, by his grace that we were granted the gift of agency, and by his grace that we were given and instructed in the plan of salvation, that is, the plan whereby we could become as he is. These singular truths are the exclusive province of Latter-day Saints. We alone embrace the faith that we are actually and literally the spirit offspring of divine parents and that we can, through the plan provided by our divine parents, obtain an exalted state like unto theirs. The theology of no other Christian faith dares offer such hope. Indeed, to them such promises are derided as blasphemous.

The divine plan required the creation of the earth so that we could be granted the privilege of coming here to obtain a physical body and be able to prove ourselves worthy to return to God's presence. The testing experience required the existence of opposites, so that we might use our agency and learn to make wise choices. Thus the earth, after its creation in a state pronounced good, or glorious, by God, was to become a telestial, or fallen, world through the transgression of Adam.

In turn this meant that all of Adam's posterity would be subject to two deaths: physical and spiritual. Physical death is simply the separation of body and spirit. Spiritual death is to be cast out of the presence of God on account of contamination by that which is unclean. Jacob, the son of Lehi, describes the role of Christ in redeeming us from the effects of these two deaths: "O the wisdom of God, his mercy and grace! For behold, if the flesh should rise no more our spirits must become subject to that angel who fell from before the presence of the Eternal God, and become the devil, to rise no more. And our spirits must have become like unto him, and we become devils, angels to a devil, to be shut out from the presence of our God, and to remain with the father of lies, in misery, like unto himself" (2 Nephi 9:8–9). Thus it was that our spirits, being tainted with sin and having no way to cleanse themselves of its effects, would be subject to the author of sin. We would become citizens of his kingdom, required to worship him without agency, knowing neither freedom nor light. Ours would be a state of perdition, for we would be hopelessly lost.

The role of Christ in redeeming us from the state described by Jacob is, like the grace of the Father, unknown to our friends in the sectarian world. That is so because they do not understand the necessity of a corporeal resurrection. Only in the inseparable union of body and spirit can we receive a fulness of joy, which is the fulness of our Father's kingdom.

Without a proper understanding of the Fall, we cannot have a proper understanding of the Atonement and Christ's grace as it is represented in that supernal event. In turn, to understand the Fall, we must understand the nature of the original creation. The knowledge of each of these principles—the Creation, the Fall, and the Atonement—are again the exclusive province of those who have embraced in faith the revelations of the Restoration.

Consider briefly how an understanding of the Creation expands our understanding of the Fall and through it our understanding of the Atonement. In the Creation all things—plants, animals, the earth, and the man, Adam, and his wife, Eve—were created in an incorruptible state. They were not subject to death, aging, pain, sorrow, or corruption in any form. They had been pronounced by their creator to be godlike. Thus when Adam fell, all things fell with him. The earth, which is a living thing, became subject to corruption and evil in all its forms as a result of Adam's fall. It was not in a fallen state when it was created by God. All plant and animal life—that which is in the heavens, and on the earth, and in the seas—became corrupted. Each was now subject to death. Each was interrupted in the pursuit of its eternal felicity. Such is the state of our fallen world, and such is the state that is rectified in and through the atonement of Christ. Because of his atonement, the earth, which is subject to death, will be resurrected and become an exalted sphere to be inhabited by those whose bodies are celestial. And as the earth will come forth into a new-ness of life, so will all living creatures that have inhabited it. Each in turn will enjoy the blessings of an exalted state. Thus the eternal world will be graced by the beauty of plants and trees, by the singing of birds, and by the companionship of animals.

The atonement of Christ extends the blessings of Christ's grace not only to all of God's children but to all of his creations. Once again we are invited to stretch our minds far beyond the bounds of traditional Christianity. Christ created worlds without number, and as such he is their Creator, and so he is their Redeemer. The declaration of this singular truth is recorded in holy writ in these words: "That by him, and through him, and of him, the worlds are and were created, and the inhabitants thereof are begotten sons and daughters unto God" (D&C 76:24). Expressing these same truths in poetic form, the Prophet wrote:

And I heard a great voice, bearing record from heav'n,
He's the Saviour, and only begotten of God—
By him, of him, and through him, the worlds were all made,
Even all that career in the heavens so broad.

Whose inhabitants, too, from the first to the last,
Are sav'd by the very same Saviour of ours;
And, of course, are begotten God's daughters and sons,
By the very same truths, and the very same pow'rs.

("A Vision," 82–83)

As all of Adam's children are natural heirs to the Fall, so all are rightful heirs to the grace of Christ in overcoming its tempo-ral effects. In the language of scripture, the corruptible will become incorruptible, meaning that death, aging, and pain will end for all. The promise is without limit or qualification. The full blessings of Christ's mercy and grace, however, become ours only through the exercise of agency. Salvation must be a matter of choice. It grows out of a covenant relationship. In making covenants, we choose to take upon ourselves the name of Christ and to keep his commandments. Conditioned upon our doing so, we are adopted his sons and daughters and become heirs, as he is an heir, to the fulness of the Father. No one can force salvation upon us, nor can blessings of such matchless worth be given to us without the consecration of our efforts in return. Thus the Lord says: "I, the Lord, am merciful and gracious unto those who fear me, and delight to honor those who serve me in righteousness and in truth unto the end" (D&C 76:5). The full measure of his mercy and grace become ours as we seek to serve him "in righteousness and in truth." Again, we have been commanded to "reconcile" ourselves "to the will of God, and not to the will of the devil and the flesh; and remember, after ye are reconciled unto God, that it is only in and through the grace of God that ye are saved" (2 Nephi 10:24). Nephi stated the principle in these words: "For we labor diligently to write, to persuade our children, and also our brethren, to believe in Christ, and to be reconciled to God; for we know that it is by grace that we are saved, after all we can do" (2 Nephi 25:23).

In so saying, I am aware that it has been argued that the word *after* in the preceding text can be interpreted as a preposition of separation rather than one of sequence—that is, that it carries the meaning "apart from" rather than "as a result of." The purpose of such an interpretation is to emphasize that the grace of God is not the crown upon our labors but rather the heart and soul of our hope of salvation. That such is the case is beyond dispute. Yet it is equally true that only those who do all that they can do can receive the fulness of God's grace. And the fulness of God's grace comes only to those who are exalted. It was never supposed that Christ atoned for the sins of the world so that we might have the option of finding some measure of happiness in the lower kingdoms. The atonement of Christ was first and foremost to bring us back into the presence of God in a glorified and exalted state. Christ atoned for our sins so that we might become as God is. We become so by advancing from grace to grace, or from one labor to a greater labor, until we have received the fulness of the Father (see D&C 93:6–20). As we comply with the laws and ordinances of the gospel, we obtain the full effects of Christ's grace in a sequential manner, for that is the manner in which we receive the ordinances of salvation.

QUESTION

What does it mean to say that we were born under the covenant? What difference does it make?

ANSWER

To be born under the covenant is to be born to parents who have been sealed by the authority of the priesthood for time and eternity. It is to be part of an eternal family. No blessing could be of greater worth to a righteous man or woman than the promise that their posterity are sealed to them, meaning they are bound together as a family, throughout the endless expanses of eternity. When loved ones are taken from us, no knowledge is more comforting than the assurance that we will know each other again in the worlds to come. So it is that the "same sociality which exists among us here will exist among us there, only it will be coupled with eternal glory, which glory we do not now enjoy" (D&C 130:2).

In addition to the blessings of the sealing power, President Joseph Fielding Smith explained that those born under the covenant "have claims upon the blessings of the gospel beyond what those not so born are entitled to receive. They may receive a greater guidance, a greater protection, a greater inspiration from the Spirit of the Lord" than those not so born (*Doctrines of Salvation,* 2:90). Those born under the covenant are rightful heirs to all the promises made to father Abraham. The Lord told him that it would be his posterity that would be privileged to hold the priesthood and minister "the blessings of salvation, even of life eternal" to those of all nations (Abraham 2:9–11). The children of the covenant have rightful claim upon all the ordinances of salvation.

Such marvelous promises are not without obligation. To be born "under covenant" is to be born with the obligations of the covenant. It is also to be born with the assurance that long before you were born, you were properly prepared for the offices, callings, and responsibilities that will be yours. Of such the scriptures declare, "even before they were born, they . . . received their first lessons in the world of spirits and were prepared to come forth in the due time of the Lord to labor in his vineyard for the salvation of the souls of men" (D&C 138:56). Young men were born with the responsibility to live worthy of the priesthood and to serve, as called, in the great missionary labor of the Church. Male and female alike are expected to consecrate their means, their time, their energy, and their talents to the building up of the kingdom of God.

QUESTION

Can those who are converts to the Church and thus were not born under the covenant receive the same blessings as those who were?

ANSWER

Certainly. It is for this purpose that families are sealed together in the temple.

QUESTION

What is believing blood?

ANSWER

Believing blood "is the blood that flows in the veins of those who are the literal seed of Abraham—not that the blood itself believes, but that those born in that lineage have both the right and a special spiritual capacity to recognize, receive, and believe

71

the truth. The term is simply a beautiful, a poetic, and a symbolic way of referring to the seed of Abraham to whom the promises were made. It identifies those who developed in preexistence the talent to recognize the truth and to desire righteousness" (McConkie, *New Witness for the Articles of Faith*, 38–39). To Abraham's seed went the promise that they would be called upon to bear the priesthood and minister for the Lord among all nations. It is for them to carry the message of salvation to all who will hear it (see Abraham 2:9, 11).

In our egalitarian age, we are constantly reminded not to think of ourselves as better than anyone else. The idea of a believing blood or a chosen people is seen as religious elitism, against which people are warned. Indeed, the notion that there is no such thing as a chosen people or believing blood is a poison that robs the life of everything that it touches. In principle that notion is no different from the notion that all churches are equally acceptable to God. To accept the idea that there can be no true church argues against the existence of God. It is to concede that there is no sure path we can follow to obtain the blessings of heaven. Similarly, to accept the idea that God has chosen none to represent him and to carry the message of salvation to the ends of the earth is to accept the idea that God has no message to send.

QUESTION

Do those who have entered into the new and everlasting covenant of marriage have the promise that they will not lose any of their children?

ANSWER

The idea of a risk-free system of salvation or an absolute assurance that none of a certain group will be lost sounds dangerously like the proposition made by Lucifer in the Grand Council of heaven whereby the salvation of all was to be assured. This does not mean, however, that there is not an inheritance of faith and blessing that we can bequeath to our children. Spiritual birthrights can be handed from generation to generation, just as physical or temporal inheritances can be handed down through the generations.

Perhaps the principle is most easily demonstrated by way of contrast. Let us ask, Can bitterness and opposition to the kingdom of God bequeath a negative inheritance to a person's children? In the dedicatory prayer of the Kirtland Temple, the Prophet asked the Lord to make bare his arm in protecting his people from enemies who had done much to afflict them. He prayed, "May thine anger be kindled, and thine indignation fall upon them, that they may be wasted away, both root and branch, from under heaven" (D&C 109:52). In response to that plea, we read in a subsequent revelation, "not many years hence, . . . they [the persecutors] and their posterity shall be swept from under heaven, saith God, that not one of them is left to stand by the wall." Of those who swore falsely against the Lord's anointed the revelation stated: "They shall not have right to the priesthood, nor their posterity after them from generation to generation" (D&C 121:15, 21).

Surely, if the blood of those who fought against the Lord is to be remembered from generation to generation, so the posterity of the faithful will be remembered in the blessings of the Lord. Again revelation sustains such a conclusion. In the dedicatory prayer of the Kirtland Temple we find the Prophet making this appeal for the faithful: "We ask thee, Holy Father, to establish the people that shall worship, and honorably hold a name and standing in this thy house, to all generations and for eternity; that no weapon formed against them shall prosper; that he who diggeth a pit for them shall fall into the same himself; that no combination of wickedness shall have power to rise up and prevail over thy people upon whom thy name shall be put in this house" (D&C 109:24–26).

Consider the language used to describe the return of the keys, or the authority, by which the eternal family unit is formed: "Elias appeared, and committed the dispensation of the gospel of Abraham, saying that in us and our seed all generations after us should be blessed" (D&C 110:12). Surely the promise of blessings to future generations spoken of here would embrace their own posterity. Indeed, it was through their posterity that future generations were to be blessed.

In the revelations of the Restoration, parents are explicitly commanded to plant faith and gospel understanding in the hearts of their children (see D&C 68:25–28; 93:40). Despite their best efforts, some children will choose to stray from their parents' teachings and example. Though their hearts will ache, faithful parents, whose children are heirs of the covenant but who have wandered, have reason to hope. Joseph Smith taught, "When a seal is put upon the father and mother, it secures their posterity, so that they cannot be lost, but will be saved by virtue of the covenant of their father and mother" (*Teachings of the Prophet Joseph Smith*, 321).

Elder Orson F. Whitney taught: "The Prophet Joseph Smith declared—and he never taught a more comforting doctrine—that the eternal sealings of faithful parents and the divine promises made to them for valiant service in the Cause of Truth, would save not only themselves, but likewise their posterity. Though some of the sheep may wander, the eye of the Shepherd is upon them, and sooner or later they will feel the tentacles of Divine Providence reaching out after them and drawing them back to the fold. Either in this life or the life to come, they will return. They will have to pay their debt to justice; they will suffer for their sins; and may tread a thorny path; but if it leads them at last, like the penitent Prodigal, to a loving and forgiving father's heart and home, the painful experience will not have been in vain. Pray for your careless and disobedient children; hold on to them with your faith. Hope on, trust on, till you see the salvation of God" (in Conference Report, April 1929, 110).

QUESTION

Will those who die before arriving at the age of accountability be saved in the highest degree of the celestial kingdom?

ANSWER

Yes. By revelation Joseph Smith was told that "all children who die before they arrive at the years of accountability are saved in the celestial kingdom of heaven" (D&C 137:10). These in their infant state are "innocent before God" (D&C 93:38). The Savior declared that "little children are whole, for they are not capable of committing sin; wherefore the curse of Adam is taken from them in me, that it hath no power over them" (Moroni 8:8).

President Joseph Fielding Smith taught, "It does not make any difference whether it is a Catholic baby, a Protestant baby, or a Mohammedan baby: no matter whose baby it is, it is not responsible for original sin; it is not responsible for any sin; and the mercy of God claims it; and it is redeemed" (Smith, *Doctrines of Salvation*, 2:53).

"Not only will little children be saved in the celestial kingdom of God, but they will be heirs of exaltation in that kingdom. (*Doctrines of Salvation*, vol. 2, pp. 49–57.) On this point the Prophet said: 'They will there enjoy the *fulness* of that light, glory and intelligence, which is prepared in the celestial kingdom.' (*Teachings*, p. 200.) To inherit the *fulness* is to have exaltation," declared Elder Bruce R. McConkie (*Mormon Doctrine*, 674–75).

Although children who die before arriving at the age of accountability will automatically inherit the highest degree of the celestial kingdom, we do not perform temple ordinances for them. Yet no one can be exalted separately and singly. Thus it would seem that at some point they will participate in the ordinances of the temple and be granted the privilege of being sealed to the companion of their choice.

Elder Melvin J. Ballard wrote this about those who die without marriage:

"You mothers worry about your little children [who have died]. We do not perform sealings for them. I lost a son six years of age, and I saw him a man in the spirit world after his death, and I saw how he had exercised his own freedom of choice and would obtain of his own will and volition a companionship, and in due time to him, and all those who are worthy of it, shall come all of the blessings and sealing privileges of the house of the Lord. Do not worry over it. They are safe; they are all right.

"Now, then what of your daughters who have died and have not been sealed to some man? . . . The sealing power shall be forever and ever with this Church, and provisions will be made for them. We cannot run faster than the Lord has provided the way. Their blessings and privileges will come to them in due time. In the meantime, they are safe" (Hinckley, *Sermons and Missionary Services of Melvin Joseph Ballard*, 260).

QUESTION

How many of our Father's children will inherit the celestial kingdom?

ANSWER

Of those who kept their first estate and gained the privilege of being born into mortality the vast majority will return to the presence of their heavenly parents to receive the fulness of their divine inheritance. In so saying I am fully aware of the scriptural declaration that "strait is the gate, and narrow is the way, which leadeth unto life, and few there be that find it" (Matthew 7:14; 3 Nephi 27:33). This declaration is directed to the world of which we are a part. It does not, however, include those who die before the age of accountability. Nor does it include those who do not have the opportunity to hear the gospel in mortality. These will be taught all principles essential to salvation in the world of the spirits and given the opportunity to embrace them there. Further, it does not include that portion of the premortal host who will live in the

Millennium, in which "children shall grow up without sin unto salvation" (D&C 45:58). Given that there will be no disease, infanticide, or premature death in that state and that people will retain their youth until they are a hundred years of age, we have every expectation that there will be a remarkable population explosion (see D&C 101:30; Isaiah 65:20). From such a perspective it can only be concluded that the great victory in numbers will be the Lord's and that he will save (meaning exalt) the greater portion of his children.

AT ISSUE

That which was created by the grace of God must find salvation in that same grace. At issue is the role mankind must play in obtaining salvation. Some have held that the decision is God's alone, that by his choice some are saved and others are not. A popular voice of our day suggests that this salvation is obtained by the profession of faith "not of works, lest any man should boast" (Ephesians 2:9). Yet another and older voice declares that salvation is found only in the sacraments and authority of the Church. As Latter-day Saints we could not profess to be the possessors of the gospel in its pristine purity and not have a plain and clear answer to this divisive issue. Indeed, the very story of the restored gospel constitutes God's response to this most important question. In May 1829, John the Baptist came to Joseph Smith and Oliver Cowdery and restored the authority to perform the ordinance of baptism by immersion for the remission of sins. Thus, even before the organization of the Church, baptism was instituted as an ordinance of salvation. With the restoration of this authority comes the announcement that faith in Christ and repentance from sin are requisites for baptism (see D&C 20:37). In penning the first three Articles of Faith, Joseph Smith announces first our faith in God, next that we will not be punished for Adam's transgression, and then that "through the Atonement of Christ, all mankind may be saved, by obedience to the laws and ordinances of the Gospel" (Article of Faith 3).

We embrace Christ both as Savior and as Lord, or Master (see 1 Nephi 22:12; 2 Nephi 6:18; 31:13). We understand that "only unto him that has faith unto repentance is brought about the great and eternal plan of redemption" (Alma 34:16). To him we bow the knee, and in his cause we seek to serve with all our heart, might, mind, and strength, that we might "stand blameless before God at the last day" (D&C 4:2). It is the firstfruits of our labors that we offer to the Lord, not that which costs us nothing (2 Samuel 24:24). We have taken upon ourselves his name, knowing that there is no other name under heaven whereby mankind might be saved.

CHAPTER FIVE

THE PREMORTAL LIFE

Because many Bible passages sustain the idea of a premortal life, why is it
that only Latter-day Saints believe in this doctrine?

Do we have any idea where we lived in our premortal, or first, estate?

Do the spirits of those yet to be born mingle with the spirits of those who
have died?

Because we lived with God in our premortal life, was faith unknown to us?

Can spirits in the premortal life hold the priesthood?

Were faithful and righteous people involved in the creation of the earth?

Were some more valiant than others in the War in Heaven?

Did sin and repentance occur in the premortal existence?

Were two plans presented at the Grand Council for God to choose
between?

Could Satan's plan to force us all to be righteous possibly have worked?
Could God have accepted it?

Did we make choices of companions and families before our mortal birth?

To what extent do our actions in the premortal existence affect who and
what we are in this life?

Did we have existence (entity and agency) before our birth as spirits?

THE DOCTRINE OF A PREMORTAL LIFE, once common to the faith of Jews and Christians alike, is now the exclusive province of Latter-day Saints. We alone bear witness that the God of heaven is actually the Father of our spirits, that we are his sons and daughters, sired in his image and likeness. We alone possess the faith that as children of divine parentage we have the capacity to become as God is and that the text declaring Adam and Eve to be in his image and likeness is literally true. We accept the plain meaning of the psalmist's words: "Ye are gods; and all of you are children of the most High" (Psalm 82:6). We believe ourselves to be children of destiny who in principle and intent have claim upon the words uttered by the Lord to Jeremiah: "Before I formed thee in the belly I knew thee; and before thou camest forth out of the womb I sanctified thee, and I ordained thee a prophet unto the nations" (Jeremiah 1:5). Extending this principle to all who are of the household of faith, the Prophet Joseph Smith said, "Every man who has a calling to minister to the inhabitants of the world was ordained to that very purpose in the Grand Council of heaven" (*Teachings of the Prophet Joseph Smith*, 365).

In our premortal estate not only were we taught the gospel but we made covenants to accept and live it when we came to earth. President Spencer W. Kimball said: "We made vows, solemn vows, in the heavens before we came to this mortal life [Abraham 3:22, 24–26].

"We have made covenants. We made them before we accepted our position here on earth.

"Now we made this commitment, '. . . all things whatsoever the Lord our God shall command us.' We committed ourselves to our Heavenly Father, that if He would send us to the earth and give us bodies and give us the priceless opportunities that earth life afforded, we would keep our lives clean and would marry in the holy temple and would rear a family and teach them righteousness. This was a solemn oath, a solemn promise. He promised us an eventful mortal life with untold privileges and providing we qualified in the way of righteousness, we would receive eternal life and happiness and progress. There is no other way to receive these rewards" ("Be Ye Therefore Perfect," 2). Thus as Latter-day Saints we believe ourselves to have been foreordained to receive all spiritual blessings, meaning all the ordinances of salvation, long before being born into mortality (see Ephesians 1:1–4).

QUESTION

Because many Bible passages sustain the idea of a premortal life, why is it that only Latter-day Saints believe in this doctrine?

ANSWER

During the second century after the birth of Christ, the Christian world adopted the doctrine of creation ex nihilo, which holds that God brought the universe into existence out of nothing. According to this doctrine, God alone called all things into existence as evidence of his goodness. Such a notion rejects the idea that matter is eternal or that anything existed in spirit form before it existed physically. Things that are spoken of as having existed before mortality are believed to have done so only in the sense of having existed in God's mind before their actual creation.

QUESTION

Do we have any idea where we lived in our premortal, or first, estate?

ANSWER

Yes. In a poem written by the Prophet Joseph Smith, we find this line: "From the council in Kolob, to time on the earth" ("A Vision," 82). If Kolob, the planet nearest to the residence of God, is where the Grand Council was held, it seems reasonable to suppose that it was also the planet upon which we resided in our premortal estate.

QUESTION

Do the spirits of those yet to be born mingle with the spirits of those who have died?

ANSWER

The idea that premortal spirits will mingle with postmortal spirits plays havoc with the doctrine that those who did not have an opportunity to accept the gospel in mortality will have that chance in the spirit world and thus "be judged according to men in the flesh" (1 Peter 4:6; D&C 138:10). Surely to be surrounded by the unborn but faithful hosts of the premortal life would more than tip the scales in favor of accepting the gospel for those who did not hear it in mortality. No faith would be necessary in such cases, for the veil of forgetfulness would have been lifted.

The labor of the unborn spirit is to prepare itself for mortality; the labor of the disembodied spirit is to prepare for resurrection and the glories of an immortal world. Perhaps those differences in purpose are themselves sufficient to suggest a difference in place.

The source used to justify the mingling of spirits from our first estate with disembodied spirits is President Joseph F. Smith's vision of the redemption of the dead (see D&C 138). This vision describes Christ's visit to the spirit world between the time of his death and his resurrection. In this vision President Smith mentions that he saw the Prophet Joseph, Hyrum Smith, Brigham Young, John Taylor, Wilford Woodruff, and others of the faithful of our dispensation. From this statement comes the assumption that these men were present at the time of Christ's visit to the spirit world in the meridian of time.

But a more careful reading of the vision does not sustain that conclusion. President Smith said that those who were present at the time of Christ's visit were those "who had been faithful in the testimony of Jesus while they lived in mortality; and who had offered sacrifice in the similitude of the great sacrifice of the Son of God, and had suffered tribulation in their Redeemer's name" (D&C 138:12–13). Some in our dispensation have certainly been faithful in the testimony of Jesus and suffered tribulation in their Redeemer's name, but it would not be accurate to say that they had offered animal sacrifice, which was in similitude of the sacrifice of Christ, which had just taken place. A list of those present when Christ appeared in the spirit world is then given (see D&C 138:38–49). It starts with Adam and Eve and mentions such notables as Abel, Seth, Noah, Shem, Abraham, Isaac, Jacob, Moses, Isaiah, Ezekiel, Daniel, Elias, Malachi, and Elijah. In addition, it notes that the Book of Mormon prophets were also present. These "had looked upon the long absence of their spirits from their bodies as a bondage" (D&C 138:50). Those present were then given the "power to come forth" from the grave after the resurrection of Christ (D&C 138:51).

There is no thought in all of this that the unborn are present. It simply doesn't fit to suppose that the unborn would be given the power of resurrection. This marvelous vision was followed by another in which President Smith saw the spirit world as it was at that time (3 October 1918). It is in this vision that he mentions seeing those of our dispensation who had died. Of them he said, "I beheld that the faithful elders of this dispensation, when they depart from mortal life, continue their labors in the preaching of the gospel" (D&C 138:57).

The change of scene, including time and place, is common to visions of this sort. Joseph Smith's vision on the degrees of glory (see D&C 76) does this same thing, as does Nephi's account of the dream both he and his father had of the tree of life (see 1 Nephi 11).

QUESTION

Because we lived with God in our premortal life, was faith unknown to us?

ANSWER

We are the sons and daughters of heavenly parents with whom we lived before our birth into mortality. In that first estate we were schooled and prepared for the challenges that this mortal probation would bring and for the special labors that would be ours. Of that premortal experience it is often said that we walked by sight, not having to exercise faith because the reality of God and his divine powers was obvious to us. That did not preclude the necessity of faith, however. Alma tells us that those destined to become faithful high priests were "called and prepared from the foundation of the world according to the foreknowledge of God, on account of their exceeding faith and good works; in the first place being left to choose good or evil; therefore they having chosen good, and exercising exceedingly great faith, are called with a holy calling, yea, with that holy calling which was prepared with, and according to, a preparatory redemption for such" (Alma 13:3). This brief statement, uttered in a single sentence, teaches volumes about our premortal life. It makes it evident that it was not a sinless or tranquil state. Evil existed, and the opportunity to make bad choices was abundant.

One-third of the host of heaven was cast out of the first estate when they rebelled and attempted to dethrone God. Faith was very much an issue, although not faith in the reality of God's existence but in the plan of salvation, which centered in the necessity of his eldest Son becoming a sinless sacrifice for the rest of us. Alma's expressions are poignant. He spoke not just of faith but of the necessity of our exercising "exceeding faith" and again of our having "exceedingly great faith."

QUESTION

Can spirits in the premortal life hold the priesthood?

ANSWER

"With regard to the holding of the priesthood in the premortal existence, I will say," stated President Joseph Fielding Smith, "that there was an organization there just as well as an organization here, and men there held authority. Men chosen to positions of trust in the spirit world held the priesthood" (in Conference Report, October 1966, 84). "There must be leaders, presiding officers, and those who are worthy and able to take command," President Smith explained further. "During the ages in which we dwelt in the premortal state we not only developed our various characteristics and showed our worthiness and ability, or the lack of it, but we were also where such progress could be observed. It is reasonable to believe that there was a Church organization there. The heavenly beings were living in a perfectly arranged society. Every person knew his place. Priesthood, without any question, had been conferred and the leaders were chosen to officiate. Ordinances pertaining to that premortal existence were required and the love of God prevailed. Under such conditions it was natural for our Father to discern and choose those who were most worthy and evaluate the talents of each individual. He knew not only what each of us *could* do, but also what each of us *would* do when put to the test and when responsibility was given us. Then, when the time came for our habitation on mortal earth, all things were prepared and the servants of the Lord chosen and ordained to their respective missions" (*Way to Perfection*, 50–51).

"The Priesthood was first given to Adam; he obtained the First Presidency, and held the keys of it from generation to generation," taught the Prophet Joseph Smith. "He obtained it in the Creation, before the world was formed" (*Teachings of the Prophet Joseph Smith*, 157). "Certainly this was also true of the other noble and great ones," stated Elder Bruce R. McConkie. "Those who sided with Christ and Adam and who joined with them in taking of the materials that existed and in making an earth—certainly they all acted in the power and authority of the same priesthood held by Jehovah and Michael" (*New Witness for the Articles of Faith*, 310).

Even Lucifer was once a holder of the priesthood of God. In the revelation on the degrees of glory, we read of him that he was once "an angel of God who was in authority" (D&C 76:25).

QUESTION

Were faithful and righteous people involved in the creation of the earth?

ANSWER

Yes. We learn this information from Abraham 3. It describes a vision depicting our first estate in which Abraham is shown an assembly of spirits described as "the noble and great ones." In number, we are told simply, there were "many." In relation to the population of the whole earth, that would have to have been a sizable number. Knowing of those whom the Lord has called upon to display both nobility and greatness, we would surmise that this number would have included both male and female spirits. In this vision Abraham was to learn that he was one of them (see Abraham 3:22–23). Further, describing this assembly the Lord said, "There stood one among them that was like unto God [obviously Christ], and he said unto those who were with him: We will go down, for there is space there, and we will take of these materials, and we will make an earth whereon these may dwell; and we will prove them herewith, to see if they will do all things whatsoever the Lord their God shall command them" (Abraham 3:24–25).

A description of the order of creation then follows in Abraham 4 and a confirmation of its completion in Abraham 5. The account begins with the Lord saying, "Let us go down. And they went down at the beginning, and they, that is the Gods [or "noble and great ones"], organized and formed the heavens and the earth" (Abraham 4:1). Later in this account we read that "the Gods took counsel among themselves and said: Let us go down and form man in our image, after our likeness; and we will give them dominion over the fish of the sea, and over the fowl of the air, and over the cattle, and over all the earth, and over every creeping thing that creepeth upon the earth. So the Gods went down to organize man in their own image, in the image of the Gods to form they him, male and female to form they them" (Abraham 4:26–27).

Why were those involved in the task of creation called Gods? Would it not be because they had been commanded to act in the name of Deity in the labor of creation? Would it not be because they were of the family of God and thus known by the name of their Father? (see Psalm 82:1–6). Would it not be because it was their destiny to become as God is through the experience of creation and the subsequent experience that would be theirs in mortality?

QUESTION

Were some more valiant than others in the War in Heaven?

ANSWER

The great confrontation between Christ and Lucifer that began in our first estate continues here on earth. One way to answer the question of whether some were more valiant than others in the conflict there is to ask, Are some more valiant than others in the same conflict here? Many in this life seek to avoid the fight. They act as if a truce had been declared between the forces of light and darkness. Indeed, their perception of the gospel is that it must be lived and taught in such a manner that offense is never given. President Marion G. Romney warned against trying to "serve the Lord without offending the devil" ("Price of

Peace," 6). We assume that the noble and great ones described in Abraham's vision (see Abraham 3:22–23) proved themselves such in the conflict between the course of good and evil.

QUESTION

Did sin and repentance occur in the premortal existence?

ANSWER

The full gospel plan existed in our premortal estate. There all its principles were taught to us (see D&C 132:11). In a revelation given to Joseph Smith we are told that "every spirit of man was innocent in the beginning; and God having redeemed man from the fall, men became again, in their infant state, innocent before God" (D&C 93:38). This text is commonly understood to mean that at the time of our birth as spirits, all the children of God were innocent and that because of the atonement of Christ we become again, in our infant state, innocent once more. Thus the atonement of Christ applies not only to those sins that are properly repented of in this life or in our postmortal life but to those committed between the time of our birth as spirits and our birth into mortality. If the gospel is the same yesterday, today, and forever, as the scriptures repeatedly tell us, then the doctrine of repentance must remain the same also (see 1 Nephi 10:18; 2 Nephi 2:4; 29:9; Mormon 9:9; D&C 20:12).

QUESTION

Were two plans presented at the Grand Council for God to choose between?

ANSWER

The great question posed by God at the Grand Council was not, "What shall I do?" God did not need instruction from his children about how they should be saved. The question was, "Whom shall I send?" (Abraham 3:27). Implicit in the question is the understanding that there is but one plan—the plan of God, a plan understood by all his spirit children, a plan that required a redeemer—and thus the matter at issue was not how we were to be saved but rather who would be chosen to act as our Savior. Thus Christ responded by saying, "Father, thy will be done, and the glory be thine forever" (Moses 4:2). That is to say, "Father, I understand your plan. I accept it and will follow it and, appropriately, the glory will be thine forever." Lucifer, on the other hand, said, "Behold, here am I, send me, I will be thy son, and I will redeem all mankind, that one soul shall not be lost, and surely I will do it; wherefore give me thine honor" (Moses 4:1). That is, "Because your plan requires a redeemer, I will be that redeemer; indeed, I will save all your children, and thus the glory should be mine." The Father said, "I will send the first," meaning his Firstborn Son, he who is known to us as Jesus of Nazareth (Abraham 3:27). It was because he was not chosen to be our Savior—the Only Begotten of the Father in the flesh—that Lucifer rebelled, not because God refused his ideas about what the plan of salvation should be.

QUESTION

Could Satan's plan to force us all to be righteous have worked? Could God have accepted it?

ANSWER

The plan of salvation was known to all long before the Grand Council was held. At issue was which of the Father's spirit children would be chosen to be his Only Begotten in the flesh. In his attempt to obtain that honor Lucifer offered to redeem "all mankind, that one soul shall not be lost, and surely I will do it; wherefore give me thine honor" (Moses 4:1). It was a universal salvation of which Lucifer spoke. He intended to save everyone, even though the Father had said that some souls would not be saved (see Smith, *Teachings of the Prophet Joseph Smith*, 357). His words contained no reference to righteousness. It is a contradiction in terms to suppose that there is such a thing as forced righteousness. Righteousness must always be a free-will offering. If there is no agency, there can be no righteousness.

QUESTION

Did we make choices of companions and families before our mortal birth?

ANSWER

We know that some were privileged to choose their companions before their birth into mortality. As illustrations we might think it only obvious that this was the case with Adam and Eve, Abraham and Sarah, Joseph and Mary, and Joseph Smith Sr. and Lucy Mack Smith. On the other hand, it is equally obvious that much of the marrying and giving in marriage that takes place in the world is lacking the inspiration of heaven. To what extent then, we would ask, have those within the household of faith been accorded this privilege? Such a question can be answered only by revelation. Some have been told, in patriarchal blessings, for instance, that their marriage was first agreed upon in heaven or that they chose their children. In most instances, even when that is the case, those involved have been required to struggle through the same kind of experiences to find their mate as have those who are without this assurance. Certainly the effort necessary to make a good marriage and a happy home is no less for them than it is for others.

It would be inappropriate for anyone to attempt to manipulate the feelings or agency of another in a courtship with the claim that it had been revealed to him or her that the couple were to be married. The very fact that someone would mention such a thing could in and of itself be sufficient proof otherwise. Were such a thing true, surely the one to whom the revelation had been given ought to trust the Lord to bring His will to pass.

QUESTION

To what extent do our actions in the premortal existence affect who and what we are in this life?

ANSWER

This question can be posed in may forms. For instance, To what extent do the experiences of youth affect adulthood? To what extent do students' study habits affect performance on tests? To what extent does athletes' training affect performance in competition? Perhaps the best comparison, in this instance, would come from asking, To what extent does what we do in this life affect who and what we will be in the life to come?

We have been told through revelation that "whatever principle of intelligence we attain unto in this life, it will rise with us in the resurrection. And if a person gains more knowledge and intelligence in this life through his diligence and obedience than another, he will have so much the advantage in the world to come" (D&C 130:18–19). This principle is a simple reflection of the justice of God. Our works, the scriptures declare, follow us into the world to come, and it will be from these same works that we are judged (see D&C 59:2; Revelation 14:13). In a very real sense we are our own judges, because what we have done and been is reflected perfectly in what we are (see Alma 41:7).

"There is a law," we are told, "irrevocably decreed in heaven before the foundations of this world, upon which all blessings are predicated—and when we obtain any blessing from God, it is by obedience to that law upon which it is predicated" (D&C 130:20–21). According to the law of God, we lay claim to blessings in the world to come by virtue of things we do in this life. That same law dictates that we have claim to blessings in this life by virtue of things done in our first estate. As what we do today will affect tomorrow, so what we did yesterday affects today. Everyone is born into this life with talents and propensities brought with them from the previous existence.

President Joseph Fielding Smith explained: "In the parable of the talents the Lord makes use of this very significant expression: 'For the kingdom of heaven is as a man traveling into a far country, who called his own servants, and delivered unto them his goods. And unto one he gave five talents, to another two and to another one; to every man according to his several ability.' Without doubt, these characteristics were born with us. In other words, we developed certain traits of character in the world of spirits before this earth-life began. In that life some were more diligent in the performance of duty. Some were more obedient and faithful in keeping the commandments. Some were more intellectual, and others manifested stronger traits of leadership than others. Some showed greater faith and willingness to serve the Lord, and from among these the leaders were chosen" (*Way to Perfection*, 50).

"Men are not born equal," said Elder Bruce R. McConkie. "They enter this life with the talents and capacities developed in preexistence. Abraham saw in vision the spirit hosts of men before they were born, 'and among all these there were many of the noble and great ones.' It was of that select and talented group that the Lord said: 'These I will make my rulers.' And to Abraham, the Father of the Faithful, one of the greatest of the Lord's earthly rulers, the comforting word came: 'Thou art one of them; thou wast chosen before thou wast born.' (Abraham 3:22–23.) Alma tells us that those who are faithful high priests in this life were in fact 'called and prepared from the foundation of the world according to the foreknowledge of God, on account of their exceeding faith and good works' while they yet dwelt in his presence. (Alma 13:3.) To Jeremiah the Lord said: 'Before I formed thee in the belly

I knew thee; and before thou camest forth out of the womb I sanctified thee, and I ordained thee a prophet unto the nations.'
(Jeremiah 1:5.)" (*New Witness for the Articles of Faith*, 34).

Because we know that all blessings are predicated on obedience to law, when individuals are born into this life with any blessing—it matters not what that blessing is—we can be confident
that they have a rightful claim to it. We can be equally confident
that they will be answerable to a just God for what they do with
the opportunities and blessings that are theirs. Even though the
Lord gives us weakness that we might be made strong (see Ether
12:27), the converse does not necessarily follow. That is, just
because individuals are born with a disability of one sort or another
or because they are born into circumstances less fortunate than
others, we cannot conclude that there has been some misbehavior
on their part before they were born. The noblest of spirits are often
placed in the sorriest of circumstances so that they might be a
blessing to others or so that through those circumstances they
might gain strength, or faith, or some other refining attribute. It is
beyond mortal ability to determine what constitutes a blessing, for
we have no way of knowing what will bring us nearest to God.

QUESTION

Did we have existence (entity and agency) before our birth as
spirits?

ANSWER

This is a question to which we simply don't have an answer. It
is one of those matters on which good people differ and perhaps
with good reasons. The idea that the spirits had entity and agency
before their spirit birth is not a doctrine of the Church and should
not be taught as such.

Two scriptural texts are generally used to justify this notion.
They are the statement in Abraham relative to God's organizing

the intelligences (supposedly the primal element) from which he chose the noble and great ones (see Abraham 3:22) and the passage in Doctrine and Covenants 93:30, which states that all truth is independent in the sphere in which God has placed it and that it can act for itself "as all intelligence also; otherwise there is no existence." A careful reading of the Abraham texts makes it clear that no allusion is made to the primal element when the word "intelligence" is used; in Abraham 3:22–23 "intelligences," "souls," and "spirits" are used synonymously. The reference to their organization is not to their creation but to their foreordination. "The Father called all spirits before Him" before their birth into mortality, Joseph Smith explained, "and organized them"; he placed Adam at the head and gave him the keys of the priesthood (*Teachings of the Prophet Joseph Smith*, 158).

A careful reading of Doctrine and Covenants 93:30 does not suggest the existence of life forms before God called them into existence. In fact, the thrust of the text is precisely the opposite. It tells us that all things exist precisely because God called them into existence. The existence of all things evidences the hand of a creator. "All truth is independent in that sphere in which God has placed it," we are told in this passage. That is to say, when God ordains a law it stands independent. It does not need to be wound up every morning or restarted. It simply operates as it was ordained to operate. As it is with laws, so it is with eternal truths. They too stand independent. Compliance with them brings the same blessings in all ages. To disregard them brings the same consequences in all ages. Were this not the case—that is, if God did not have this power—there would be neither God nor existence, for his justice and mercy would then vary from age to age.

At Issue

Our knowledge of the premortal life comes to us through revelation and the teachings of our modern prophets. Though the Old and New Testaments allude many times to the doctrine of our premortal existence, without the aid of modern revelation and the understanding given us by our living oracles, we would no more understand these references than do our sectarian friends.

Our understanding of the premortal existence is also greatly expanded by the knowledge that all gospel principles are eternal and that to understand how they apply in this life is to understand at the same time how they applied in ages past and how they will apply in ages future. To know how the gospel functions or the kingdom of God operates here and now is to know how it functioned in the premortal life, how it functions in the spirit world, and how it will function in the worlds to come.

CHAPTER SIX

LIFE BEYOND THE GRAVE

Will it be harder or easier to embrace the gospel in the spirit world?

How is it that Peter said Christ visited the spirits in prison and yet
President Joseph F. Smith said He did not go among the wicked? (see
1 Peter 3:19; D&C 138:20–23).

Does Christ's promise to the thief on the cross that he would be with Him
in paradise sustain the idea of deathbed repentance?

Are spirit prison and hell the same place?

Is there repentance in spirit prison?

What did Alma mean when he said "the spirits of all men, whether they be
good or evil, are taken home to that God who gave them life"? (Alma
40:11).

What is the book of life out of which we will be judged?

At death do we receive a restoration of our memory of the premortal
existence?

Do only baptized members of the Church go to paradise?

Can it properly be said that if someone goes to paradise at death, his or her
calling and election is made sure?

Is there resurrection for those who become sons of perdition in this life?

After the resurrection, can we advance from degree to degree so that

someone who was telestial can eventually become terrestrial
and someone who was terrestrial become celestial?
Do Gods continue to learn throughout eternity?
What do the scriptures teach about eternal progression?
Do we have guardian angels?

AS LATTER-DAY SAINTS WE POSSESS a host of revealed truths—some from dispensations past, others unique to our own—which give meaning, purpose, consolation, and hope in that which will be when we or a loved one leaves this sphere of existence. With these revelations as a source, we can respond to many questions about life beyond the grave.

QUESTION

Will it be harder or easier to embrace the gospel in the spirit world?

ANSWER

If God is just, then all of his children must have an equal opportunity to accept or reject the gospel before the Day of Judgment. As Latter-day Saints, we know that those who did not have the opportunity to accept the gospel in this life will have it in the spirit world before they are called forth from the grave. These, Peter said, will then "be judged according to men in the flesh" (1 Peter 4:6). This statement means that the standard of discipleship is the same in this world and in the next.

In a revelation given to Joseph Smith, we learn that there was a law, "irrevocably decreed in heaven before the foundations of this world, upon which all blessings are predicated—and when we obtain any blessing from God, it is by obedience to that law upon which it is predicated" (D&C 130:20–21). There is no place that we can go to escape the laws of God or their effects. Those laws applied in our premortal life, they apply in mortality, and they will apply in the spirit world and in the eternities to come. The God we worship is "infinite and eternal, from everlasting to everlasting the same unchangeable God, the framer of heaven and earth, and all things which are in them" (D&C 20:17). When the scriptures speak of an everlasting gospel, they are describing a gospel that is everlastingly the same (see D&C 27:5; 101:39).

In principle it should be neither easier nor harder to exercise faith or to repent in the spirit world. Were that not the case, those in that estate could not be judged according to men in the flesh. For some it will be natural and easy to accept and live gospel truths, for that will have been the practice of a lifetime. For others it will be very difficult to do so, for eschewing the things of the Spirit will have been the practice of a lifetime. The difference is not in the gospel but in the hearts and souls of those to whom the message is being presented.

We must allow, however, for circumstances in which people were prisoners to experiences in this life that prevented them from having a fair chance to embrace gospel principles here. When they are freed from those bitter chains, many of them will seek the blessings of the gospel.

QUESTION

How is it that Peter said Christ visited the spirits in prison and yet President Joseph F. Smith said He did not go among the wicked? (see 1 Peter 3:19; D&C 138:20–23).

ANSWER

The phrase "spirit prison" as used in the scriptures refers to the entire spirit world. "Spirit prison" embraces both paradise and the place of torment to which wicked spirits are consigned. For instance, Enoch, speaking of the morning of the first resurrection, said: "The saints arose, and were crowned at the right hand of the Son of Man, with crowns of glory; and as many of the spirits as were in prison came forth, and stood on the right hand of God; and the remainder were reserved in chains of darkness until the judgment of the great day" (Moses 7:56–57). Both those who were crowned with glory on the right hand of God and those who were confined to "chains of darkness" are spoken of by Enoch as being in prison.

The reason those in paradise are spoken of as being in prison or as being prisoners is made plain by President Joseph F. Smith in the vision of the redemption of the dead. Speaking of the righteous who were awaiting the arrival of Christ, he said, "While this vast multitude waited and conversed, rejoicing in the hour of their deliverance from the chains of death, the Son of God appeared, declaring liberty to the captives who had been faithful" (D&C 138:18). In this text the captives awaiting deliverance are righteous souls. It is to them that Christ declared liberty, and it was for them he broke the bands of death that they might be freed from the "chains of death." Even in the spirit world they could be freed from the effects of Adam's fall, including the separation of body and spirit, only in and through Christ's atoning sacrifice. So it was that "the dead had looked upon the long absence of their spirits from their bodies as a bondage" (D&C 138:50; 45:17).

Thus we have Peter speaking of the visit of Christ to those in spirit prison (see 1 Peter 3:18–20) and Joseph F. Smith telling us that He went only to those who were in paradise (see D&C 138:20–23). Both paradise and what we are in the habit of calling hell are part of spirit prison.

QUESTION

Does Christ's promise to the thief on the cross that he would be with Him in paradise sustain the idea of deathbed repentance?

ANSWER

No. In fact, as Joseph Smith explained, Christ said no such

thing. *Paradise* is a modern word (meaning "garden") that does not answer to the original word used by the Savior. *Paradise* is used in two other instances by the King James translators. In all three cases the text is sufficiently ambiguous to defy any meaningful definition (see Luke 23:43; 2 Corinthians 12:4; Revelation 2:7). Said the Prophet, "There is nothing in the original word in Greek from which this was taken that signifies paradise; but it was—This day thou shalt be with me in the world of spirits: then I will teach you all about it and answer your inquiries" (*Teachings of the Prophet Joseph Smith*, 309). Thus the thief on the cross was being promised neither salvation nor a place among the redeemed. The promise given him was that he would have the opportunity to be taught the gospel in the spirit world.

As to the word *paradise*, the Prophet used it in the Book of Mormon to mean "a state of happiness, which is called paradise, a state of rest, a state of peace, where they [the righteous] shall rest from all their troubles and from all care, and sorrow" (Alma 40:12). *Paradise* is used only twice in the Doctrine and Covenants: the first appears to be as a synonym for *heaven*, and the second means the place of departed spirits before the resurrection (see D&C 77:2, 5).

Teaching these principles, Elder Orson Pratt explained how the thief on the cross "turned to Jesus in his expiring moments, and said unto him, Lord, remember me when thou comest into thy kingdom. And Jesus said unto him—'Verily I say unto thee, Today shalt thou be with me in paradise.' And where is that? Is it in the kingdom of God? Let us inquire into this matter. We find that paradise, according to the definitions given by the most eminent writers, is a place of departed spirits. Where did Jesus go? Peter said he went to preach to the spirits in prison, while his body was in the tomb. The Church of England, in one of their articles, say that Jesus Christ suffered death and descended into hell, and after three days he rose again and ascended to his Father. What did he go there for? Peter says to preach the Gospel to them that were dead, that they might be judged according to men in the flesh. Did the thief go with him? Yes: 'This day shalt thou be with me in paradise;' and there I will preach to you among the rest. But to enter the mansion where God dwells, and where the holy angels dwell, you must be born of water and of the Spirit, or you cannot enter that kingdom. Adam could not go there; Enoch could not; Abraham, Isaac, Jacob, Moses, and the Prophets, none of them could get into that kingdom without being born of water and the Spirit. This astonished Nicodemus; and Jesus said—'Art thou a master of Israel, and knowest not these things?'—as much as to say, the new birth had been unfolded to the people since the beginning of man, and handed down from generation to generation, and yet you are 'a master in Israel,' and do not know these things! It was the only way of salvation before Jesus came, and it was the only way after he came. And these ordinances must be administered by properly authorized persons" (in *Journal of Discourses*, 7:264–65).

QUESTION

Are spirit prison and hell the same place?

ANSWER

The spirit world and spirit prison are one and the same place. The general thought seems to be that the phrase "spirit prison" equates with hell or the place of torment. Such a conclusion, however, does not accord with scripture. Peter tells us that upon His death Christ went and "preached unto the spirits in prison" (1 Peter 3:19). President Joseph F. Smith in his vision of the redemption of the dead tells us that Christ did not go to the ungodly or the unrepentant but to a vast assembly of the righteous. These, he said, were "rejoicing in the hour of their deliverance from the chains of death." The revelation then says that "the Son of God appeared, declaring liberty to the captives who had been faithful" (D&C 138:18). The promise that the prison of death would end comes to the righteous in and through Christ, who would redeem them from the dead. "For the dead had looked upon the long absence of their spirits from their bodies as a bondage" (D&C 138:50), and as long as they remained in that state they could not receive a fulness of joy (see D&C 93:33–34).

Until we are resurrected we bear the burden of Adam's fall. We are prisoners of death, and hence the name "spirit prison" serves appropriately as a designation for the entire spirit world. As a part of his vision Enoch saw that Saints would arise and be crowned "at the right hand of the Son of Man, with crowns of glory," and then he added, "And as many of the spirits as were in prison came forth, and stood on the right hand of God; and the remainder [of those in prison] were reserved in chains of darkness until the judgment of the great day" (Moses 7:56–57).

Joseph Smith explained: "Hades, the Greek, or Sheol, the Hebrew, these two significations mean a world of spirits. Hades, Sheol, paradise, spirits in prison, are all one; it is a world of spirits. The righteous and the wicked all go to the same world of spirits until the resurrection" (*Teachings of the Prophet Joseph Smith*, 310).

In common speech, however, *hell* is generally used to denote the place of torment for the wicked. The LDS Bible Dictionary (699) notes, however, that in both the Jewish and Christian faiths "Hades (meaning broadly the place of all departed spirits) consists of two parts, *paradise* and *Gehenna*, one the abode of the righteous and the other of the disobedient." For instance, Peter, commenting on one of the psalms, said of Christ that his soul would not be "left in hell" (Acts 2:31)—that is, his spirit would not remain forever in the world of the spirits. This passage is an affirmation that the resurrection embraces the reunion of body and spirit. In the Book of Mormon, *hell* always refers to the place of torment or the abode of the wicked. The revelations in the Doctrine and Covenants use the word in the same manner.

QUESTION

Is there repentance in spirit prison?

ANSWER

A proper understanding of what spiritual progress can be made in the world of spirits must be founded on the declaration of Amulek, who said: "This life is the time for men to prepare to meet God; yea, behold the day of this life is the day for men to perform their labors. And now, as I said unto you before, as ye have had so many witnesses, therefore, I beseech of you that ye do not procrastinate the day of your repentance until the end; for after this day of life, which is given us to prepare for eternity, behold, if we do not improve our time while in this life, then cometh the night of darkness wherein there can be no labor performed. Ye cannot say, when ye are brought to that awful crisis [death], that I will repent, that I will return to my God. Nay, ye cannot say this; for that same spirit [disposition] which doth possess your bodies at the time that ye go out of this life, that same spirit [disposition] will have power to possess your body in that eternal world" (Alma 34:32–34).

Amulek is teaching us that death does not change a person's nature, nor does it change how close the person is to God. If it has become our nature to resist the things of the Spirit in this life, such will be our nature in the world to come. If, on the other hand, we have developed a propensity for spiritual things in this life, we carry that propensity with us into the spirit world. We know, as the scriptures declare, that our works follow us (see 3 Nephi 27:12; D&C 59:2; Revelation 14:13).

The principles that determine who will be granted the opportunity to exercise faith, repent, accept ordinances performed vicariously in their behalf, and receive the fulness of gospel blessings were announced in a marvelous vision given to Joseph Smith on 21 January 1836. The Lord said, "All who have died without a knowledge of this gospel, who would have received it if they had been permitted to tarry, shall be heirs of the celestial kingdom of God; also all that shall die henceforth without a knowledge of it, who would have received it with all their hearts, shall be heirs of that kingdom" (D&C 137:7–8).

What was announced here is that only those who die without the opportunity to hear the gospel while in the flesh will have the opportunity to receive the fulness of its blessings in the world to come. Others may hear the gospel again in the spirit world and choose to accept it there, but having rejected it when it was first brought to them in mortality, they have forfeited the opportunity to receive the fulness of its blessings (see D&C 76:74). Emphasizing this principle in a poem, Joseph Smith wrote:

> They receiv'd not the truth of the Saviour at first;
> But did, when they heard it in prison again
>
> ("A Vision," 84)

Thus in the spirit world the fulness of gospel blessings goes to those who died without the opportunity to receive them in mortality and who God judges would have received them "with all their hearts" (D&C 137:8) if that opportunity had come to them. That is to say, they would have been true and faithful in all things. The principles involved evidence the justice of God. Those who receive the gospel in the spirit world do so as if they were in the flesh. The requisite faith, obedience, and courage associated with accepting the gospel can be no less there than it is here in mortality (see D&C 138:10). There are no shortcuts to the kingdom of heaven. The price appended to its blessings remains constant from dispensation to dispensation and from one world to the next.

QUESTION

What did Alma mean when he said "the spirits of all men,

whether they be good or evil, are taken home to that God who gave them life"? (Alma 40:11).

ANSWER

If those who have not heard the gospel are taken back into the presence of God at the time of death, they would have a decided advantage in accepting it when it was taught to them in the spirit world. If that were the case, they could not be judged according to men in the flesh, as the scriptures tell us they will be (see 1 Peter 4:6; D&C 138:10). Alma later tells us that "there is a space between death and the resurrection of the body, and a state of the soul in happiness or in misery until the time which is appointed of God that the dead shall come forth, and be reunited, both soul and body, and be brought to stand before God, and be judged according to their works" (Alma 40:21). We see then that Alma does not expect the judgment to take place before the resurrection, and therefore a judgment before a resurrection could not be what he has in mind when he says that the spirits of all men will be taken home to the God who gave them life.

Perhaps what Alma has in mind with the expression "taken home to God" is that they will in a broad and general sense be in his presence, though he will not personally manifest himself to any that he would not have manifested himself to had they remained in the flesh. King David expresses the same sentiment in this language: "Whither shall I go from thy spirit? or whither shall I flee from thy presence? If I ascend up into heaven, thou art there: if I make my bed in hell, behold, thou art there. If I take the wings of the morning, and dwell in the uttermost parts of the sea; even there shall thy hand lead me, and thy right hand shall hold me" (Psalm 139:7–10).

QUESTION

What is the book of life out of which we will be judged?

ANSWER

It will be from the body we obtain at the time of our mortal birth that we will be judged. It is here that we will write our book of life. The knowledge of all that we have done—or left undone, as the case may be—is recorded in our body and soul. Every feeling, thought, and action combine to determine who and what we are on the day of resurrection. "They who are of a celestial spirit shall receive the same body which was a natural body; even ye shall receive your bodies, and your glory shall be that glory by which your bodies are quickened" (D&C 88:28).

The same principle applies to those who are terrestrial, telestial, or perdition. Individuals will be rewarded according to their own works and the desires of their heart. They need not have been perfect to obtain a celestial resurrection, but the propensity and desire for the things of the Spirit must have been the dominant force in their life. Thus the scriptures say: "Ye who are quickened by a portion of the celestial glory shall then receive of the same, even a fulness" (D&C 88:29). In like manner, we read, "they who are quickened by a portion of the terrestrial glory shall then receive of the same, even a fulness. And also they who are quickened by a portion of the telestial glory shall then receive of the same, even a fulness. And they who remain shall also be quickened; nevertheless, they shall return again to their own place, to enjoy that which they are willing to receive, because they were not willing to enjoy that which they might have received" (D&C 88:30–32).

The likening of the resurrected body to a book is a most apt analogy. Though the vicissitudes of life are imposed upon us, the way we react to them is a matter of personal choice. Thus each of us writes our own history. Mistakes will be made. The choice to make corrections or not to make them rests with each of us.

QUESTION

At death do we receive a restoration of our memory of the pre-mortal existence?

ANSWER

If the sacred truths of heaven are dispensed in this life according to the preparation we have made, we can have every assurance that the same will be the case in the spirit world. The memory of our premortal experience will be revealed to us only as we are worthy to receive it. This means that some will never have that knowledge restored to them. The idea that at death our memory of the premortal existence is restored to us disrupts any notion that the blessings of the gospel are dispensed there as they are here or, as Peter said it, "according to men in the flesh" (1 Peter 4:6).

Alma teaches the principle involved: "It is given unto many to know the mysteries of God; nevertheless they are laid under a strict command that they shall not impart only according to the portion of his word which he doth grant unto the children of men, according to the heed and diligence which they give unto him. And therefore, he that will harden his heart, the same receiveth the lesser portion of the word; and he that will not harden his heart, to him is given the greater portion of the word, until it is given unto him to know the mysteries of God until he know them in full. And they that will harden their hearts, to them is given the lesser portion of the word until they know nothing concerning his mysteries; and then they are taken captive by the devil, and led by his will down to destruction. Now this is what is meant by the chains of hell" (Alma 12:9–11).

QUESTION

Do only baptized members of the Church go to paradise?

ANSWER

Speaking of those who did not have the opportunity to comply with the ordinances of the gospel in this life, Joseph Smith said, "Every man that has been baptized and belongs to the kingdom has a right to be baptized for those who have gone before; and as soon as the law of the Gospel is obeyed here by their friends who act as proxy for them, the Lord has administrators there [in the world of spirits] to set them free" (*Teachings of the Prophet Joseph Smith*, 367).

It will be remembered that Christ spoke of the division in the spirit world in his parable about the rich man and Lazarus. At death Lazarus was carried by the angels to Abraham's bosom while the selfish rich man died and went to hell. No longer could the two communicate, for the Savior said that between them a great gulf was fixed. When the rich man asked that Lazareth be sent to bring him a drop of water, his request was refused because there was no association between those in Abraham's bosom, or paradise, and those in the place of torment (see Luke 16:9–31).

The description given by President Joseph F. Smith of those present when Christ visited the spirit world states that the righteous were "gathered together in one place." Those gathered are described as the "just, who had been faithful in the testimony of Jesus while they lived in mortality." Further, we are told that all of these "had offered sacrifice in the similitude of the great sacrifice of the Son of God," which ordinances to be acceptable would have required officiators who held the priesthood, and that they "had suffered tribulation in their Redeemer's name," which again assumes that they had taken that name upon them by way of gospel covenant (D&C 138:12–13).

The real problem here is that it seems unjust to consign to a place of torment those of a terrestrial spirit or, more particularly, those who are of a celestial nature but who have not yet had the opportunity to hear and accept the gospel. Should such be consigned to a place of suffering? To so suppose obviously does not accord with the justice of God. The concern is resolved in a more complete understanding of the nature of the spirit world. It is not eternal burnings. Such language is simply figurative. Certainly some will be in a state of eternal torment, but not everyone will be. Hell is simply the nation of departed spirits. Its cities have their ghettoes but also their pleasant suburbs. Kindred spirits by nature gather together. Where honorable men and women have gathered, honor prevails. Where people of peace, virtue, and goodness choose to assemble, there such attributes will also be found. Others unlike them would be unwelcome and would seek society among those of like spirit. The scriptures assure us that our works will follow us after death. Men and women of goodness here will be of the same nature there and enjoy the fruits of their labors even as they await the day when they will be taught the gospel.

QUESTION

Can it properly be said that if someone goes to paradise at death, his or her calling and election is made sure?

ANSWER

Yes. No one apostatizes from paradise. Abraham taught the principle thus: "And they who keep their first estate shall be added upon; and they who keep not their first estate shall not have glory in the same kingdom with those who keep their first estate; and they who keep their second estate shall have glory added upon their heads for ever and ever" (Abraham 3:26). The Book of Mormon prophets speak of this life as a time of probation. When the time comes to depart this life and go to paradise, we are no longer on probation. Thus Alma counseled us to "keep your garments spotless, that ye may at last be brought to sit down with Abraham, Isaac, and Jacob, and the holy prophets who have been ever since the world began, having your garments spotless even as their garments are spotless, in the kingdom of heaven *to go no more out*" (Alma 7:25; emphasis added). The phrase "just men made perfect" is used to describe individuals who have obtained this status. That is, they are men and women whose lives were such that they are justified to expect that in the resurrection they will be made perfect (see D&C 76:66–69; 129; Hebrews 12:22–23).

QUESTION

Is there resurrection for those who become sons of perdition in this life?

ANSWER

Yes. Doctrine and Covenants 88, the great revelation on resurrection for our dispensation, tells us that after all others have been resurrected, the fourth trump will sound and those who are "filthy still," that is, those who cannot obtain a degree of glory, will be resurrected; these "shall return again to their own place," meaning hell, or outer darkness (D&C 88:102, 32).

Confusion about the resurrection of sons of perdition may be the result, at least in part, of misunderstanding two verses in the revelation on the degrees of glory. There we read that those who will be perdition are the "only ones on whom the second death shall have any power" and the "only ones who shall not be redeemed"; "all the rest shall be brought forth by the resurrection of the dead" (D&C 76:37–39). The second death is separation from the presence of God. It is not denial of a resurrection. It is banishment to outer darkness. To be redeemed is to be freed from the dominion and power of Satan. Those who are perdition will know no such freedom. Joseph Smith taught that all who have bodies will have power over those who do not (see *Teachings of the Prophet Joseph Smith*, 181). Thus Cain will rule over Satan in the world to come (see Moses 5:23, 30). As to the phrase in Doctrine and Covenants 76:39, "For all the rest shall be brought forth by the resurrection," it is interesting to note that in an early copy of the revelation, this phrase reads "who shall be brought forth" (*The Evening and the Morning Star* 1, no. 2 [July 1832]: [2]).

QUESTION

After the resurrection, can we advance from degree to degree so that someone who was telestial can eventually become terrestrial and someone who was terrestrial become celestial?

ANSWER

If the resurrection is the inseparable union of body and spirit, advancing from degree to degree would be impossible. It would defy the meaning of words to suppose that an inseparable union of a telestial spirit and a telestial body could be changed for something either better or worse. To argue such a possibility would be to argue at the same time that exalted beings were subject to apostasy and that our probationary estate was never ending.

The revelations describe resurrection as the union of body and spirit "never to be divided" (Alma 11:45; D&C 138:17). Furthermore, they tell us that "where God and Christ dwell" those who are telestial "cannot come, worlds without end" (D&C 76:112). Those who do not obtain an exaltation in the celestial kingdom will not be gods but "angels of God forever and ever" (D&C 132:17). "The righteous shall be gathered on my right hand unto eternal life," the Lord said, "and the wicked on my left hand will I be ashamed to own before the Father; wherefore I will say unto them—Depart from me, ye cursed, into everlasting fire, prepared for the devil and his angels. And now, behold, I say unto you, never at any time have I declared from mine own mouth that they should return, for where I am they cannot come, for they have no power" (D&C 29:27–29).

QUESTION

Do gods continue to learn throughout eternity?

ANSWER

No. Ignorance and godhood are incompatible. To suppose that God is infinitely learning is to also suppose him to be infinitely ignorant. At issue is whether God is eternally a student or not. All scripture and the Prophet Joseph Smith teach of a God who has all knowledge, all power, and all wisdom. In the *Lectures on Faith* the Prophet said, "If it were not for the idea existing in the minds of men that God had all knowledge it would be impossible for them to exercise faith in him" (Lecture 4:11). Hyrum Smith said, "I would not serve a God who had not all wisdom and all power" (Smith, *History of the Church*, 6:300).

QUESTION

What do the scriptures teach about eternal progression?

ANSWER

The phrase "eternal progression" is not found in the scriptures, nor do we find it in the sermons and writings of Joseph Smith. There are obvious difficulties in announcing as doctrine a concept that is without scriptural basis.

The scriptures emphatically declare God to have all knowledge both in heaven and on earth (see Psalm 147:4–5; John 16:30; 1 Nephi 9:6; 2 Nephi 2:24; 9:20; Mosiah 4:9; Alma 7:13; 26:35; Mormon 8:17; Moroni 7:22; Moses 1:6; D&C 38:1–2; 88:7–13, 41). Further, they promise the faithful that they will receive the fulness of the Father (see D&C 93:19–20). "He that keepeth his commandments receiveth truth and light, until he is glorified in truth and knoweth all things" (D&C 93:28).

The scriptures teach that God continues to advance in glory

through the exaltation of his children (see Moses 1:39). They also teach that we can continue to grow in understanding and godliness in the spirit world (see D&C 93:19; 138:58–59). The idea that there is advancement within the different kingdoms of glory is speculative.

QUESTION

Do we have guardian angels?

ANSWER

Without question there are occasions upon which those from the other side of the veil reach out to bless and protect those of us in mortality. Numerous scriptural texts attest to such a thing. Of those who keep their covenant to magnify the priesthood, the Lord said, "I have given the heavenly hosts and mine angels charge concerning you" (D&C 84:42). Of his missionaries he said: "Whoso receiveth you, there I will be also, for I will go before your face. I will be on your right hand and on your left, and my Spirit shall be in your hearts, and mine angels round about you, to bear you up" (D&C 84:88). Of those who have been endowed in the temple and have received the promised blessing of protection there, the Lord said they would go forth from his house armed with power and his name would be upon them, his glory round about them, and, he added, "angels have charge over them" (D&C 109:22).

Nonetheless, the notion that each of us has a particular angel assigned to us with the sole responsibility to follow us around "silent notes taking" is not good doctrine (*Hymns*, no. 237). Such a thought is demeaning to both the living and the dead. It demeans the living in the assumption that we need constant watching, a divine baby-sitter, as it were. It demeans the dead in the assumption that they have no greater work or labor to do. That simply is not the case. Were it so, we would be left to wonder why we had been given the companionship of the Holy Ghost and a blessing of protection as part of the endowment.

AT ISSUE

If one possesses the faith that there is life beyond the grave, the central questions then become: What is the nature of that life? Does death profoundly change our nature? and Is the world of departed spirits significantly different from this one? Properly, the revelations of the Restoration answer these questions, for as Joseph Smith said, "If we have any claim on our Heavenly Father for anything, it is for knowledge on this important subject" (*Teachings of the Prophet Joseph Smith*, 324).

In all matters of importance we know that life beyond the grave is an extension of this one. "That same sociality," the Prophet told us, "which exists among us here will exist among us there, only it will be coupled with eternal glory, which glory we do not now enjoy" (D&C 130:2). As to the question of whether death changes our nature, Amulek said, "That same spirit [disposition] which doth possess your bodies at the time that ye go out of this life, that same spirit [disposition] will have power to possess your body in that eternal world" (Alma 34:34). Regarding how that world differs from this, we can but say that if this life is a preparation for the one to follow, then there must be a natural transference of experiences gained here. Otherwise, we could not correctly say that our works follow us in the world to come or that intelligence obtained in this life is of value or worth in the world to come.

CHAPTER SEVEN

SIGNS OF THE TIMES AND THE MILLENNIAL DAY

Will the Second Coming be in the year 2000?

How close are we to the Second Coming?

How large will the Church be when Christ comes?

Is Christ waiting for the members of his Church to become sufficiently righteous before he returns?

Will the faithful be called on to walk back to Missouri?

In the Millennium, will righteous mothers be able to rear children who died before maturity?

Are false Christs a serious threat in the Christian world today?

We are told in the scriptures that in the last days Christ will "suddenly come to his temple" (Malachi 3:1; 3 Nephi 24:1). In our day we have many temples and the prophetic promise that temples will be built in both the New Jerusalem and the Old Jerusalem. To which temple will Christ "suddenly" come?

Aren't the ten tribes together in a body waiting for the instruction to return?

Doesn't the creation of the state of Israel in 1948 and the return of the Jews to the Holy Land constitute one of the most important signs of the times?

FOR THE WORLD THE COMING OF Christ will, in the imagery of the scriptures, be as a thief in the night. They will be caught unaware. For the Latter-day Saints, however, that should not be the case. We have been given many prophetic signs of the times by which we are to know, if not the day and hour, surely the approximate time of the Lord's coming. For us the coming of Christ is to be as it is with the woman in travail, that is, the expectant mother in labor. Though the moment of birth is not known to her, the blessed event will neither be a surprise nor come too soon (see 1 Thessalonians 5:2–8; D&C 106:4–5).

As we move closer to the time of the Second Coming, ours becomes a world increasingly "filled with all manner of lyings, and of deceits, and of mischiefs, and all manner of hypocrisy, and murders, and priestcrafts, and whoredoms, and of secret abominations" (3 Nephi 16:10). It will be, we are told, a day of false Christs, false prophets, and false doctrines. It will be a day in which the Prince of Darkness will gather his multitudes upon the face of the earth among all the nations of the Gentiles to fight against the Lamb of God. So evil will things become that our only promise of protection will be in keeping the sacred covenants we have made and in being "armed with righteousness and with the power of God" (1 Nephi 14:14).

QUESTION

Will the Second Coming be in the year 2000?

ANSWER

Not according to Doctrine and Covenants 77. In his great apocalyptic vision, John the Revelator gives a prophetic description of the seven thousand years of earth's temporal history (see Revelation 5–10). While laboring on his translation of the Bible, Joseph Smith recorded a revelation explaining John's writings (see D&C 77). Both that revelation and the revelation of John along with Doctrine and Covenants 88 affirm that earth's temporal history, contrary to all scientific theories, is confined to what John called seven seals, or seven thousand-year periods. It is generally thought by Latter-day Saints that Christ will return at the beginning of the final, or seventh, thousand-year period. This idea may have given rise to the notion that he will come in the year 2000, based on the understanding that there were four thousand years from the fall of Adam to the birth of Christ (see the Chronology chart in the LDS Bible Dictionary, 635) and that we are approaching the year 2000 after the birth of Christ. Thus six thousand years of earth's temporal history will have been completed and the stage set for the seventh thousand-year period, or the time of Christ's millennial reign.

Yet, in the Doctrine and Covenants we read: "In the beginning of the seventh thousand years will the Lord God sanctify the earth, and complete the salvation of man, and judge all things, and shall redeem all things, . . . and the sounding of the trumpets of the seven angels are the preparing and finishing of his work, in the beginning of the seventh thousand years—the preparing of the way before the time of his coming" (D&C 77:12). Rather than welcome Christ at this time, we are told, we will begin the preparations for his coming. The revelation, which takes the form of questions and answers, then asks, "When are the things to be accomplished, which are written in the 9th chapter of Revelation?" which describes the wars and plagues to be poured out during the seventh seal. The Lord answered, "They are to be accomplished after the opening of the seventh seal, *before the coming of Christ*" (D&C 77:13; emphasis added). Again we are told that the coming of Christ and the beginning of the seventh seal are not synonymous.

QUESTION

How close are we to the Second Coming?

ANSWER

The question cannot be answered by turning to a calendar. It can only be answered in terms of the events that have been prophesied to take place before Christ's return. After the coming forth of the Book of Mormon and the restoration of the gospel, the most important event to precede the Second Coming is the declaration of the restored gospel throughout the nations of the earth (see Joseph Smith–Matthew 1:31; Moses 7:62). John the Revelator promised that the message of the restored gospel would go to "every nation, and kindred, and tongue, and people" through the Book of Mormon (Revelation 14:6; D&C 133:37). In a revelation to Joseph Smith, we are told that everyone will be privileged to hear the fulness of the gospel "in his own tongue, and in his own language" by legal administrators (D&C 90:11). Alma tells us that "the Lord doth grant unto all nations, of their own nation and tongue, to teach his word" (Alma 29:8). In describing the vision shown to him and his father, Nephi tells us that there will be congregations of the Saints "upon all the face of the earth" before Christ's return (1 Nephi 14:12). John the Revelator tells us that before that day, there will be those among "every kindred, and tongue, and people, and nation" who have found redemption through Christ and have been ordained "kings and priests" (Revelation 5:9–10), meaning they had received the fulness of temple blessings.

This chain of thought suggests not only that the restored gospel must be freely taught among the Arab nations, for example, but that it must be taught in their native tongues by Arabs who are legal administrators of the gospel. It further requires that there be Latter-day Saint congregations throughout all Arab nations and that there be those in their congregations who have received the fulness of temple blessings. Some considerable time will be necessary for such promises to be fulfilled. It also suggests that we have a considerable labor ahead of us and that missionary work is still in its infancy.

QUESTION

How large will the Church be when Christ comes?

ANSWER

Not only will the gospel be taught in all the world before the Second Coming but there will be congregations of the Saints among all the peoples of the earth. This suggests a Church vastly larger than at present. It must be remembered, however, that Nephi in describing his vision of the last days said that the numbers of those in the Church would be "few" and their dominions "small" (1 Nephi 14:12). "Few" and "small" take on meaning only when compared to something else. If we take as our point of reference the six members with which the Church was organized in the spring of 1830, then by comparison we have a very sizable number. But Nephi's point of comparison is the population of the whole earth. Let us suppose, for instance, that the world population is six billion at the time Christ comes and that only ten percent of that number have chosen to embrace the gospel. That would mean there would be 600 million members of the Church when Christ came. If one in five people joined the Church, or twenty percent of the population in a world of six billion, there would be 1.2 billion members of the Church—and yet in comparison with those who had not joined the Church, their numbers could quite properly be described as few and their congregations small. It may be helpful to remember that Nephi grew up in a society in which virtually everyone he associated with was of the house of Israel.

Another indication that Nephi saw in vision a sizable number is that the mother of abominations found it necessary to "gather together multitudes upon the face of all the earth, among all the nations of the Gentiles, to fight against the Lamb of God" (1 Nephi 14:13). The need to assemble an army of such size throughout all the nations of the earth would hardly exist if the population of the Church were of no consequence.

We have learned that the size of the Church in Old Testament times was appreciably larger than had generally been supposed. For instance, Alma speaks of an "exceedingly great many, who were made pure and entered into the rest of the Lord their God" (Alma 13:12). President Joseph F. Smith, in his vision of the redemption of the dead, spoke of "an innumerable company" and a "vast multitude" of faithful Saints worthy to greet the Savior when he made his three-day visit to the spirit world (D&C 138:12, 18).

As to the last days, Daniel, describing Christ's return, says that a "thousand thousands ministered unto him, and ten thousand times ten thousand stood before him" (Daniel 7:10), "which is to say an innumerable host" (McConkie, *Promised Messiah,* 611). In the great apocalypse of the New Testament, John the Revelator describes the same scene, saying, "I beheld, and, lo, a great multitude, which no man could number, of all nations, and kindreds, and people, and tongues, stood before the throne, and before the Lamb, clothed with white robes, and palms in their hands" (Revelation 7:9).

Surely from such texts we can confidently say that there will be a sizable number of faithful Saints on the earth when Christ returns, a number that vastly exceeds our present Church membership.

QUESTION

Is Christ waiting for the members of his Church to become sufficiently righteous before he returns?

ANSWER

The scriptures describe a state of wickedness that will usher in the Millennium, not a state of righteousness. Malachi speaks of the time of Christ's return as "the great and dreadful day" (Malachi

4:5), one in which the proud and the wicked shall be burned as stubble. In modern revelation we learn that Christ will come clothed in red, for his garments will appear as if they had been dyed in the wine-vat. He will say, "I have trodden the wine-press alone, and have brought judgment upon all people; and none were with me; and I have trampled them in my fury, and I did tread upon them in mine anger, and their blood have I sprinkled upon my garments, and stained all my raiment; for this was the day of vengeance which was in my heart" (D&C 133:50–51). An earlier revelation describes this as a time of lamentation:

"And there shall be weeping and wailing among the hosts of men. . . .

"And it shall come to pass, because of the wickedness of the world, that I will take vengeance upon the wicked, for they will not repent; for the cup of mine indignation is full; for behold, my blood shall not cleanse them if they hear me not.

"Wherefore, I the Lord God will send forth flies upon the face of the earth, which shall take hold of the inhabitants thereof, and shall eat their flesh, and shall cause maggots to come in upon them;

"And their tongues shall be stayed that they shall not utter against me; and their flesh shall fall from off their bones, and their eyes from their sockets;

"And it shall come to pass that the beasts of the forest and the fowls of the air shall devour them up.

"And the great and abominable church, which is the whore of all the earth, shall be cast down by devouring fire, according as it is spoken by the mouth of Ezekiel the prophet, who spoke of these things, which have not come to pass but surely must, as I live, for abominations shall not reign" (D&C 29:15–21).

Many like passages could be quoted, but the idea is clear that it will be a wicked, not a righteous, world that greets the returning Christ. It is true that Nephi says the righteousness of the people will bind Satan (see 1 Nephi 22:26), but the context is millennial, so we know that this event follows the destruction of the wicked. The story Nephi is telling in that passage is one in which the Saints are saved by divine intervention and Satan is bound by the power of the priesthood. Nephi is teaching us that the Millennium can be brought in only by the power of God, thereafter to be maintained by the righteousness of the people (see 1 Nephi 22:15–17; D&C 45:55). This sequence of events has been known at least from the days of Enoch, to whom the Lord said: "As I live, even so will I come in the last days, in the days of wickedness and vengeance, to fulfil the oath which I have made unto you concerning the children of Noah; and the day shall come that the earth shall rest, but before that day the heavens shall be darkened, and a veil of darkness shall cover the earth; and the heavens shall shake, and also the earth; and great tribulations shall be among the children of men, but my people will I preserve" (Moses 7:60–61). Thus Enoch describes "the day of the righteous" and "the hour of their redemption" as taking place in the Millennium, when he and those of his city will join those preserved by the power of God (Moses 7:67).

Though a state of wickedness will usher in the Millennium and the return of Christ, a sizable number of faithful Saints will be prepared to meet him. Describing these events, Nephi said he "beheld the power of the Lamb of God, that it descended upon the saints of the church of the Lamb, and upon the covenant people of the Lord, who were scattered upon all the face of the earth; and they were armed with righteousness and with the power of God in great glory" (1 Nephi 14:14).

QUESTION

Will the faithful be called on to walk back to Missouri?

ANSWER

This is a classic Mormon myth. No scriptural justification can be given for it. It is true that a temple will yet be built in Jackson

County, Missouri, which city will become the administrative headquarters for the Church. That does not mean, however, that all the faithful must live there or that those who go must arrive on foot.

During the time of Joseph Smith and Brigham Young, it was necessary for members of the Church to gather to Zion for both spiritual and physical safety. This is not necessary in our day, nor is it desirable. Temples are now being built throughout the world, and the Saints in many nations are able to participate in all the programs of the Church. For some years now members of the Church throughout the world have been asked to remain in their homelands to build up the Church where they live. Elder Bruce R. McConkie made that point in an area conference in Mexico City, and President Harold B. Lee repeated his statement for the direction of the whole Church in a subsequent general conference: "The place of gathering for the Mexican Saints is in Mexico; the place of gathering for the Guatemalan Saints is in Guatemala; the place of gathering for the Brazilian Saints is in Brazil; and so it goes throughout the length and breadth of the whole earth. Japan is for the Japanese; Korea is for the Koreans; Australia is for the Australians; every nation is the gathering place for its own people" (in Conference Report, April 1973, 7).

In his vision of the last days Nephi saw congregations of the Saints "upon all the face of the earth" and said that they "were armed with righteousness and with the power of God in great glory" (1 Nephi 14:12, 14). Describing the Church in the millennial day, Isaiah used the imagery of a tent: "Enlarge the place of thy tent, and let them stretch forth the curtains of thy habitations; spare not, lengthen thy cords and strengthen thy stakes; for thou shalt break forth on the right hand and on the left, and thy seed shall inherit the Gentiles and make the desolate cities to be inhabited" (3 Nephi 22:2–3; Isaiah 54:2–3).

In Doctrine and Covenants 45:66 the New Jerusalem is called "a land of peace, a city of refuge, a place of safety for the saints of the Most High God." We are further told that "the glory of the Lord shall be there, and the terror of the Lord also shall be there, insomuch that the wicked will not come unto it, and it shall be called Zion. And it shall come to pass among the wicked, that every man that will not take his sword against his neighbor must needs flee unto Zion for safety. And there shall be gathered unto it out of every nation under heaven; and it shall be the only people that shall not be at war one with another. And it shall be said among the wicked: Let us not go up to battle against Zion, for the inhabitants of Zion are terrible; wherefore we cannot stand. And it shall come to pass that the righteous shall be gathered out from among all nations, and shall come to Zion, singing with songs of everlasting joy" (D&C 45:67–71).

The language of this text in the Doctrine and Covenants seems somewhat at odds with the passages from Isaiah and 3 Nephi quoted above. There we speak of the dispersal of the righteous throughout the nations of the earth, whereas the text in the Doctrine and Covenants implies a gathering of the righteous to Jackson County, the center stake of Zion. This apparent discrepancy is resolved in the principle that all revelation is subject to interpretation by the light of subsequent revelation. For instance, Doctrine and Covenants 115:6 tells us that the gathering upon "the land of Zion, and upon her stakes, may be for a defense, and for a refuge from the storm, and from wrath when it shall be poured out without mixture upon the whole earth." Joseph Smith further told us that Zion "consists of all N[orth] & S[outh] America but that any place where the Saints gather is Zion which every righteous man will build up for a place of safety for his children" (Jessee, "Joseph Smith's 19 July 1840 Discourse," 392; see also Smith, *Teachings of the Prophet Joseph Smith*, 362).

QUESTION

In the Millennium, will righteous mothers be able to rear children who died before maturity?

ANSWER

We find the following recorded in the *History of the Church:* "Sister M. Isabella Horne said: 'In conversation with the Prophet Joseph Smith once in Nauvoo, the subject of children in the resurrection was broached. I believe it was in sister Leonora Cannon Taylor's house. She had just lost one of her children, and I had also lost one previously. The Prophet wanted to comfort us, and he told us that we should receive those children in the morning of the resurrection just as we laid them down, in purity and innocence, and we should nourish and care for them as their mothers. He said that children would be raised in the resurrection just as they were laid down, and that they would obtain all the intelligence necessary to occupy thrones, principalities and powers. The idea that I got from what he said was that the children would grow and develop in the Millennium, and that the mothers would have the pleasure of training and caring for them, which they had been deprived of in this life'" (*History of the Church*, 4:556 n).

QUESTION

Are false Christs a serious threat in the Christian world today?

ANSWER

Every once in a while some deluded soul comes along proclaiming himself to be either Christ or the Holy Ghost. These pretenders receive little attention and fade from the scene quickly. It seems evident from the scriptures that Christ's principal concern in warning about false Christs in the last days was with false ideologies or false doctrines relative to himself and his redemptive role—that is, false systems of salvation. His warning anticipates that in the last days there would be a great proliferation of messengers professing to speak in the name of the Lord while teaching all manner of foolish and false doctrines.

In a prophetic description of the promised Messiah, Isaiah said "his visage" would be more "marred" than that of any man (Isaiah 52:14). Though no mortal man has endured what Christ did in his matchless labor of atonement, the effect of his suffering was not such that it distorted his appearance in a manner to justify this prophecy. Significantly, the resurrected Christ gave a dual meaning to these words by applying them to another servant of the Lord in the last days (see 3 Nephi 20:44). We understand that servant to be Joseph Smith, who died a martyr's death, though not in a manner to distort his appearance, either. This evidence suggests that the distortion of image spoken of by Isaiah may refer to the manner in which the promised servant and his labors were to be misinterpreted and misperceived. Surely, the image of no one in earth's history has been as often or as completely distorted as that of Jesus of Nazareth. In like manner, Joseph Smith was promised that his name (image or visage) would be had for both good and evil among all nations and peoples of the earth (see Joseph Smith–History 1:33).

More has been written about Christ in the last two decades than in the previous two thousand years—most of it false. In such sources Christ has been "portrayed as a Marxist who provides the blueprints for an economic and social reform; as a Black Messiah who stood against an exploitative white nation, Rome, as a liberator who proclaimed that God's Kingdom belongs to the poor; and as the Prince of Peace who shows the way for nuclear disarmament" (Charlesworth, *Jesus within Judaism*, 26). Along with being the special advocate of the revolutionary and the social reformer, Christ has been depicted as a magician, a charismatic teacher, and a "marginal" Jew who argued with the religious leaders of the day.

The idea, it seems, is to assimilate Jesus into the image and likeness of one's own ambitions. Thus he becomes the model for peasants and kings, celibates and fathers, pacifists and soldiers, hermits and gentlemen, feudal lords and revolutionaries. For some he is the gentle shepherd-teacher; for others he is the rod of iron with which they seek to beat their opponents into submission.

Eschewing the idea that any authority or commission is necessary to speak in the name of Christ, many have taken it upon themselves to promise salvation to anyone willing to accept their right to teach his gospel and profess his grace. Others suppose themselves to be his authorized representatives—who alone can perform the ordinances of salvation—by virtue of a priesthood saturated with the blood of the Saints and soiled with endless evils. Still others, declaring him to be incomprehensible and unknowable, assume that any course of action that suits their fancy is acceptable to him. All such deny the principle of revelation by which Christ would direct the actions of any who legitimately represented him.

In another sense, false Christs are persons or organizations that profess the power to liberate us from whatever bondage they assure us we are in. Korihor, the great antichrist in the Book of Mormon, sought to liberate the Nephite people from what he called their foolish traditions and from the influence of their leaders (see Alma 30:13, 23, 24, 27).

QUESTION

We are told in the scriptures that in the last days Christ will "suddenly come to his temple" (Malachi 3:1; 3 Nephi 24:1). In our day we have many temples and the prophetic promise that temples will be built in both the New and the Old Jerusalem. To which temple will Christ "suddenly" come?

ANSWER

Malachi recorded the promise that in the last days the Lord, the messenger of the covenant, "shall suddenly come to his temple" (Malachi 3:1). This promise has been affirmed in modern revelation (see 3 Nephi 24:1; D&C 36:8; 133:2; Joseph Smith–History 1:36). It is also a matter of revelation that two of the most important signs of the times are the building of temples in the

Jerusalem of old and in the New Jerusalem, or Jackson County, Missouri (see Isaiah 2:2–3; D&C 84:2–4; 133:12–13; Ether 13:8–12). Speaking of the Jerusalem of old, Joseph Smith said, "Judah must return, Jerusalem must be rebuilt, and the temple, and water come out from under the temple, etc.; and all this must be done before the Son of Man will make His appearance" (*Teachings of the Prophet Joseph Smith*, 286). In restoring the prophecy of Enoch relative to these events, the Prophet recorded these words: "And righteousness will I send down out of heaven; and truth will I send forth out of the earth, to bear testimony of mine Only Begotten; his resurrection from the dead; yea, and also the resurrection of all men; and righteousness and truth will I cause to sweep the earth as with a flood, to gather out mine elect from the four quarters of the earth, unto a place which I shall prepare, an Holy City, that my people may gird up their loins, and be looking forth for the time of my coming; for there shall be my tabernacle, and it shall be called Zion, a New Jerusalem" (Moses 7:62).

Along with the dramatic and sudden appearance of the Lord to these two very visible and symbolic temples, we have every expectation that the Lord will visit each building so dedicated and do so frequently.

QUESTION

Aren't the ten tribes together in a body waiting for the instruction to return?

ANSWER

No. This is another classic Mormon myth. Four fundamental principles preclude such a possibility:

First, the doctrine of a universal apostasy. We simply cannot have it both ways. We cannot argue that the apostasy was universal on the one hand and that it did not include the ten tribes on the other. If the apostasy was universal, then no people remained unaffected by it. The idea that somewhere a group of people retained the faith, kept the priesthood, and had prophets is simply incompatible with the idea of an apostasy that covers the whole earth.

It has even been argued that the ten tribes are no longer on the earth and thus remained unaffected by the apostasy here. This argument is sustained by quoting Deuteronomy 30:4: "If any of thine be driven out unto the outmost parts of heaven, from thence will the Lord thy God gather thee, and from thence will he fetch thee." We have it from Joseph Smith, who held the keys of the gathering, that the phrase "outmost parts of heaven" means "the breadth of the earth" (*Teachings of the Prophet Joseph Smith*, 85).

Second, the doctrine of a universal restoration. That is, the "restoration of all things," as spoken by the "mouths of all the holy prophets since the world began" (D&C 27:6; see also Acts 3:21; D&C 86:10). The promise that "all things" are to be restored affirms that "all things" were lost. You can hardly restore the priesthood or any of its offices if that priesthood and its offices are already here. Repeatedly the scriptures tell us that the restored gospel must go to every nation, kindred, tongue, and people. Again, we cannot have it both ways. We cannot claim the divine commission to gather Israel out of every nation, kindred, tongue, and people and at the same time argue that they have not been scattered among every nation, kindred, tongue, and people.

As to teaching the gospel in our dispensation, the Lord has said that the first should be last and the last should be first. That is, that the Jew to whom the gospel was first taken in the meridian dispensation will be the last to whom it will be taken in this dispensation. Ours is the day of the Gentile, to whom we now take the gospel (see 1 Nephi 13:42). By *Gentile*, the prophetic writers mean those not of the house of Judah. Most of them will be Israelite by descent (as declared in patriarchal blessings) but Gentile by culture.

Third, Moses appeared to Joseph Smith and gave him the

"keys of the gathering of Israel from the four parts of the earth, and the leading of the ten tribes from the land of the north" (D&C 110:11). Keys are the "right of presidency," or the authority by which one presides. If the authority to preside over these events rests with Joseph Smith and his successors—this is, if they are in a position to govern the kingdom of God in all the earth—then they cannot rest with another people or other prophets. Only the president of The Church of Jesus Christ of Latter-day Saints has the authority to bring these events to pass. Missionaries are sent out by the president of the Church to gather Israel. If you want to know where Israel is, simply watch where the president of the Church sends missionaries.

Fourth, virtually hundreds of scriptures state the message, in language that is both plain and absolute, that Israel is to be gathered from the four quarters of the earth. Consider this text in 3 Nephi 5:24–26: "And as surely as the Lord liveth, will he gather in from the four quarters of the earth all the remnant of the seed of Jacob, who are scattered abroad upon all the face of the earth. And as he hath covenanted with all the house of Jacob, even so shall the covenant wherewith he hath covenanted with the house of Jacob be fulfilled in his own due time, unto the restoring all the house of Jacob unto the knowledge of the covenant that he hath covenanted with them. And then shall they know their Redeemer, who is Jesus Christ, the Son of God; and then shall they be gathered in from the four quarters of the earth unto their own lands, from whence they have been dispersed; yea, as the Lord liveth so shall it be. Amen."

This may well be the most emphatic text in all of holy writ. No other text begins and ends with the announcement that if what it is saying is not so, then God does not exist. Thus we can only conclude that if Israel is not gathered from all the face of the earth, that is, if they are somewhere in a body simply waiting to come back, then there is no God.

In Doctrine and Covenants 133:26–34 we are told that the

tribes of Israel will in a future day "come in remembrance before the Lord; and their prophets shall hear his voice" and lead them back to the "boundaries of the everlasting hills," where they shall be crowned with blessings by the children of Ephraim. This is simply to say that after missionaries have gathered them to the waters of baptism, bestowed the blessings of the restored gospel upon them, and established the Church in their midst, they will be organized according to the pattern of the Church. Inspired leaders will be called from among their number, as has been the case wherever the gospel has been taken. At the appropriate time the president of the Church—he who holds the keys of the gathering of Israel and the leading of the ten tribes from the land of the north—will direct the leaders, or prophets, who serve under his direction among the various congregations of Israel to bring their people to the temples of the Lord that they might be crowned with glory and receive the fulness of gospel blessings (see D&C 42:11).

Relative to the prophetic promises that we will receive scriptural records from the ten tribes and "all the nations of the earth" (2 Nephi 29:12), it must be understood that those records, like all revelation, must come through the proper channels. When the ten tribes return, the scriptural records they bring with them will be the Bible, the Book of Mormon, the Doctrine and Covenants, and the Pearl of Great Price. The very purpose of the Book of Mormon is to gather Israel, of which, obviously, the ten tribes are a large part. The record and testimony of the progenitors of the ten tribes will go to their descendants as the Book of Mormon is going to the descendants of Lehi.

QUESTION

Doesn't the creation of the state of Israel in 1948 and the return of the Jews to the Holy Land constitute one of the most important signs of the times?

ANSWER

The gathering of Israel as spoken of in the scriptures is destined to take place under the direction of the priesthood. Let it be stated again that the keys of the gathering of Israel rest with the president of The Church of Jesus Christ of Latter-day Saints. They do not rest with the United Nations or with any other politically appointed body. The gathering spoken of by the ancient prophets is to be first to Christ and the saving principles of his gospel and only then to lands of inheritance. Salvation is found in covenants, not in geography. Faith, repentance, baptism, and the reception of the Holy Ghost are and ever will be the first principles of any nation or kingdom established by the true God of Israel.

Israel was scattered anciently when she broke the covenants of salvation that she had made with her God, and she will be gathered only when she returns to those sacred covenants. Lands of inheritances are simply an outward, or physical, token of those covenants. Jacob taught:

"After they have hardened their hearts and stiffened their necks against the Holy One of Israel, behold, the judgments of the Holy One of Israel shall come upon them. And the day cometh that they shall be smitten and afflicted.

"Wherefore, after they are driven to and fro, . . . many shall be afflicted in the flesh, and shall not be suffered to perish, because of the prayers of the faithful; they shall be scattered, and smitten, and hated; nevertheless, the Lord will be merciful unto them, that *when they shall come to the knowledge of their Redeemer, they shall be gathered together again to the lands of their inheritance*" (2 Nephi 6:10–11; emphasis added).

Yet again, Jacob said: "Wherefore, because of their iniquities, destructions, famines, pestilences, and bloodshed shall come upon them; and they who shall not be destroyed shall be scattered among all nations.

"But behold, thus saith the Lord God: *When the day cometh that they shall believe in me, that I am Christ, then have I covenanted with their fathers that they shall be restored in the flesh, upon the earth, unto the lands of their inheritance*" (2 Nephi 10:6–7; emphasis added).

Nephi taught the same principles: "Wherefore, the Jews shall be scattered among all nations; yea, and also Babylon shall be destroyed; wherefore, the Jews shall be scattered by other nations.

"And after they have been scattered, and the Lord God hath scourged them by other nations for the space of many generations, yea, even down from generation to generation *until they shall be persuaded to believe in Christ, the Son of God,* and the atonement, which is infinite for all mankind—and when that day shall come that they shall believe in Christ, and worship the Father in his name, with pure hearts and clean hands, and look not forward any more for another Messiah, then, at that time, the day will come that it must needs be expedient that they should believe these things.

"*And the Lord will set his hand again the second time to restore his people* from their lost and fallen state. Wherefore, he will proceed to do a marvelous work and a wonder [the coming forth of the Book of Mormon and the organization of his Church] among the children of men.

"*Wherefore, he shall bring forth his words unto them,* which words shall judge them at the last day, *for they shall be given them for the purpose of convincing them of the true Messiah. . . . [And] his name shall be Jesus Christ, the Son of God*" (2 Nephi 25:15–19; emphasis added).

The present gathering of Jews to Palestine may be preparatory to the events spoken of in scripture, but it certainly does not fulfill them. It is a gathering for spiritual, not temporal, purposes of which the scriptures speak.

AT ISSUE

The first and perhaps most common misconception relative to the millennial day is simply how close we are to it. The time cannot be properly estimated in days, months, or years. It must be measured in events, the chief of which is the extent to which the gospel has been taught among the nations of the earth. Suffice it to say, so much still needs to be done before the promise is fulfilled that the gospel will be taken to those of every nation, kindred, tongue, and people that we can safely say that we are generations removed from the final winding-up scene.

The second most common misconception relative to the Millennium centers in the idea that it will take place as soon as we are sufficiently righteous. Such a conclusion contradicts the many scriptural passages that identify the return of Christ as a day of wrath and vengeance, a day of cleansing. It is to be at a time of wickedness, not of righteousness. There will, of course, be many faithful Saints scattered throughout the world who will be prepared to receive the returning Christ, but their righteousness will not hasten that which is fixed (see McConkie, *Millennial Messiah*, 26, 405).

The Millennium is a day of sanctification, of cleansing. It is a period in which the earth will rest from the sin and wickedness of the present day. It is a time in which Satan will be bound by the power of the priesthood, the gospel declared, and all things restored to their proper and perfect state. Things hidden from before the foundation of the earth will be revealed, the continents will unite into one land, the lost tribes will be restored, and faithful parents will be granted the privilege of rearing children who died in infancy.

The time of Christ's return has been known to the Father from the beginning (see Matthew 24:36). We have no power either to hasten that day or to delay it.

CHAPTER EIGHT

WOMEN AND THE PRIESTHOOD

Do we learn any distinctive or important truths about the role of women
   from the restored gospel?

The doctrine of the Church holds that spiritual gifts and the keys to the
   mysteries of the kingdom are accessible through the Melchizedek
   Priesthood. Are women less eligible than men to exercise spiritual gifts
   and to comprehend the mysteries of the kingdom?

Was it necessary for the Relief Society to be organized before women could
   receive the temple endowment? Could there be more to Relief Society
   than most Church members understand?

If women cannot hold the priesthood, how can they have authority to
   function in their Church callings? Can they have authority apart from
   the priesthood? For instance, by what authority do female temple
   ordinance workers perform ordinances?

How do we explain women giving blessings to the sick in Nauvoo?

Why can a man be sealed to more than one wife but a woman can't be
   sealed to more than one man?

How will women who do not marry and have children in mortality spend
   eternity?
How much individual life and personality is a wife and mother "allowed"
   to have? How can one determine when it is all right to put her own
   needs first? Or is it never all right?
Is it better for a woman to remain single all her life than to marry outside
   the Church?

IN RECENT YEARS EFFORTS HAVE BEEN made within the Church to
become more sensitive to the role of women. Overall, this has
been a very positive and wholesome thing, though some of these
efforts need to be increased and others redirected. There is no
question about the equality that exists between the man and the
woman in the gospel of Jesus Christ. No one has said it better than
the apostle Paul: "Neither is the man without the woman, neither
the woman without the man, in the Lord" (1 Corinthians 11:11).
It is true that the priesthood bearer presides but never without the
sustaining vote of the sisters. The gospel assumes a social equality
among all who have embraced it. As God loves us all, so we are all
to love one another. All receive the same ordinances of salvation
and do so on the same terms, thus obtaining the same promise of
blessings both in this life and in the life to come. No one within
the Church assumes office or position; there is no campaigning.
We serve when and where we are called and surrender whatever
authority we held when we are released. Our service is always on
behalf of others, never to aggrandize ourselves. The organization
of the Church cannot function without faithful women any more
than it can function without faithful men or perpetuate itself without children.

   The man and the woman are equally yoked in the responsibility to love and sustain each other, to save their families, and to
build up the kingdom of God. Too often the woman's role has been
confined to changing diapers, teaching children, preparing food,
and doing the washing. With the exception of teaching children,

we could hardly suppose that such is the role for which they were prepared and ordained in the councils of heaven.

The wake of the woman's movement has measurably altered the place of women in the theology and practice of many Christian churches in recent years. This alteration has not been simply a matter of women presiding over congregations as bishops and ministers but has resulted in a reinterpretation of the very nature of God and a rewriting of scripture. Indeed, the woman's reformation, now in its early stages, may well bring about a far greater division in traditional Christianity than that caused in the Protestant Reformation centuries ago by Martin Luther, John Calvin, and others. At issue here is whether the vine of Christianity is being pruned or uprooted.

It would be nice to cling to the naive notion that the essential issue revolves around such statements as Paul's instruction to the Corinthian Saints that "women keep silence in the churches" (1 Corinthians 14:34). Such issues are easy enough to resolve; we need simply distinguish between what is timely and what is time-less—between what is appropriate for a time and a season as dictated by the culture of a given people and what is absolute and eternal and thus the standard among the Lord's people in all ages.

No one is confused by Paul's instruction that members of the church "greet all the brethren with an holy kiss" (1 Thessalonians 5:26). If we were to attempt to follow such instruction today, no one would dare go to church, regardless of which gender was doing the preaching. As to Paul's statement about women keeping silent, it must have had reference to presiding because he expressly says that they were to both pray and prophesy (see 1 Corinthians 11:5). Paul's statements that women were not to speak in church were changed by the Prophet to read "rule," meaning "preside," in his inspired translation of the Bible (see JST 1 Corinthians 14:34, 35).

The concern of those in the front ranks of the gender battle is that if we pray to God as "Our Father in Heaven," we are conceding that God is male and that such a concession implies that maleness equals power. For those reasoning in this manner, it is essential that God be without gender and that all scriptural texts that portray God as masculine be neutralized. These are not innocuous changes. To change the way we address God also changes the God we are addressing. There is an immeasurable difference between our having been created in the image and likeness of a heavenly Father and our being the scion of "Eternal Wisdom" or "Eternal Justice." Family reunions just aren't going to be the same.

Of singular importance here is the matter of who is creating whom. Are we the children of God, or is he the child of our perceptions? Is it for us to refashion God so that we might not be embarrassed by him as our own intellectual fashions change? Such is the position of many liberal theologians today. They argue for a historical or progressive revelation of the divine nature that ignores the plain meaning of the language of scripture. This, they claim, is necessary to show respect for "individual creativity and cultural development" (Coakley and Palin, *Making and Remaking of Christian Doctrine*, 178). Plainly stated, such liberal theologians are telling us that God is what man chooses to have Him be and that we are not to take seriously such declarations as that made by the Lord to Joseph Smith in which He described Himself as being "infinite and eternal, from everlasting to everlasting the same unchangeable God, the framer of heaven and earth, and all things which are in them" (D&C 20:17).

Those who have chosen to redefine the nature of God and then to redefine the meaning of words or to rewrite scripture to accord with what they have done have reached well beyond a reformation of the church. They have changed gods and in so doing have changed the whole system of salvation. According to such theology God would no longer be our Father in Heaven, we would no longer be his sons and daughters, no longer could we suppose that we were created in his image and likeness, no longer would Christ hold place as his Only Begotten in the flesh, and no longer would Mary have claim as his mother. Our perception of resurrection would entirely change, as would our notion of what it means to assume the divine nature or to return to God's presence. We could liken all this to a business takeover in which the old name is preserved for goodwill, but everything else gets changed. All that is missing here is a sign that says "Under New Management."

Not that we haven't seen this process before. The men had their turn at the Council of Nicaea, at which philosophical speculation replaced the plain meaning of scripture, Christ became his own Father, and the gospel plan was transformed into an incomprehensible mystery. It could be argued that in fairness women ought now to have their chance to create a god and a theology too, but there are a couple of things that we ought to be reminded of. First, when the men took to creating their own god at the council of Nicaea, the result was the Dark Ages and endless woe. History demonstrates that no blessings are to be found in worshipping idols, be they made of stone or philosophical wanderings. Second, without a correct understanding of the nature of God, there can be no correct understanding of the nature of either man or woman, and if men and women don't understand who they are, their children won't understand who *they* are, either. Without the knowledge of who you are, it can hardly be expected that you will be able to find the way to your eternal home.

It is not nor can it ever be the lot of Latter-day Saints to remain neutral in any meaningful theological struggle. Outspoken leaders in the women's movement view the Church as an enemy because of the patriarchal nature of our doctrines and the idea that there are divinely appointed roles for both the man and the woman. The gender movement has claimed from among our number some converts who are filled with zeal and are anxious to reform the Church after the pattern of their sectarian counterparts who are "reforming" traditional Christianity. They seem to be oblivious to the effects of the medicine they are attempting to force down our throats.

This is not just a matter of whether a woman can hold the priesthood and be called to serve as a bishop. It involves the very nature of the God we worship. If we are going to start praying to "Our Mother in Heaven," we too are going to have to rewrite our scriptures and make fundamental changes in our theology. The salutation with which we address God is the key with which we unlock the door of heaven. Anyone who has attempted to unlock a door with the wrong key can quickly grasp the problem here. We have been repeatedly commanded to pray to the Father and to do so in the name of the Son. These are key words which have been cut to fit the lock. That is, they are in harmony with a host of other theological principles. For someone to say, "Well, I'm not going to pray the way we have been instructed. I am going to pray to our Mother in Heaven" is no different from someone saying, "Well, I am going to cut my own key. I am going to get into heaven on the merits and mercies of my Heavenly Mother, or Mary, or some other sainted woman. She will be the hope of my salvation rather than the Son of God." It is to be hoped that we will catch ourselves at this point and recognize that something in all this sounds too much like a scenario we have heard before, one that hardly represented light and truth.

To dramatize what is involved here, let us play with the notion that it does not matter whether we pray to our Father or to our Mother in Heaven because what we are attempting to obtain is a perfect equality between men and women. Then let us consider why a woman couldn't confess her sins to the bishop's wife instead of to the bishop. Surely she would better understand the problem from a woman's point of view. Now if the bishop's wife has the authority to remit sins (shared equally with her husband), surely she should also have the authority to call and release people from positions in the ward. The reason for this is obvious: She has insight, as a woman, that her husband, as a man, does not have.

Aren't husband and wife supposed to be one, anyway? Obviously it would be discriminatory to limit the right of shared authority to the bishop's wife, so all women of necessity should be entitled to the authority of their husband's office (and, of course, their husband to theirs). To assure that we do not discriminate against those women who are not married, we would also have to extend to them the same authority.

The difficulty is certainly apparent: when everyone in the ward has obtained perfect equality in authority, there is no longer any authority. Every man, woman, and child has become a bishop unto him or herself.

It might be argued that civil government shows the flaw in our illustration because it does not matter whether the mayor is a man or woman: the city government still functions. That is true. The difference is, however, that no one is arguing that the mayor's spouse has been discriminated against because he or she was not elected or appointed to that office. The spouse of the mayor enjoys equality because he or she has the same rights and privileges of citizenship as the mayor. So it is in the Church and kingdom of God. All according to their obedience are entitled to the same rights, privileges, and blessings. These blessings stand independent of office and callings. They are not exclusive to the priesthood. All become "equal" with God "in power, and in might, and in dominion" (D&C 76:95). They enjoy the fulness of all that the Father has (see D&C 93:19–20). City government again provides an illustration. If we want something done, we petition the mayor, not the mayor's spouse. We do not suppose that an injustice has been done because the spouse does not share the mayor's authority.

The theological issues, however, reach much deeper than the matter of whom the Lord chooses to hold the priesthood or other offices and callings. It embraces the matter of order and discipline necessary even in heavenly realms. Beyond that, it embraces the matter, as it does with the sectarian world, of the nature of God himself. As already noted, the woman's reformation movement takes offense at the notion of a God who has gender. Though individuals may speak of God as a personal being, such language is used only in a figurative sense. The idea of God as a person in a literal sense is simply not acceptable to them. Mormon converts to this woman's reformation movement are not necessarily interested in surrendering the idea that they actually have a Father in Heaven; what they want to do is ensure the standing and stature their Mother in Heaven has as his equal. The difficulty is the assumption that our Father in Heaven has not, either in dispensations past or to this point in the present dispensation, given our Mother in Heaven her proper due. It would appear that she, like her earthly counterparts, has been held in subjection while the Father and his sons have maintained control over everything. That is not a very flattering view of God. It would be natural enough to suppose that if Deity has been a little negligent in giving women their proper due, he has been a bit negligent in other areas also. Perhaps the gospel has become a little old-fashioned and needs some changes so that it accords more appropriately with our times. Again we return to the truth that to change the way we address God is to change the God we are addressing.

QUESTION

Do we learn any distinctive or important truths about the role of women from the restored gospel?

ANSWER

Certainly. Latter-day Saint theology is based on the premise that there was an apostasy—indeed, a universal apostasy—from the gospel as declared by all the prophets from dispensations past. Inherent in such a declaration is the fact that an understanding of the divinely appointed role of women has also been lost. Let us briefly consider some of the marvelous truths relative to the role of woman that have been restored through the Prophet Joseph

Smith. We begin with the story of creation. Adam, we are told, was born "the son of God" (Moses 6:22). Eve, his companion, came to earth in a like manner. It was because God made them "male and female," Christ explained, that a man was to leave his "father and mother" and cleave to his wife, that they twain might be one flesh (Matthew 19:4–5). Such has been the divine order from the days of Adam (see Moses 3:24).

So Adam and Eve left "father and mother," departed from Eden, and commenced life together in this fallen world. They did so as husband and wife, having been married by their divine Father. We know that their marriage was intended to be eternal, for death did not exist at the time they were sealed together. The scriptures evidence their marriage to have been one of unity, love, and oneness. It provides the pattern for the marriages of all their children. Consider, for instance, this language from the book of Moses: "And Adam and Eve, his wife, called upon the name of the Lord, and *they* heard the voice of the Lord from the way toward the Garden of Eden, speaking unto *them*, and *they* saw him not; for *they* were shut out from his presence. And he gave unto *them* commandments, that *they* should worship the Lord *their* God, and should offer the firstlings of *their* flocks, for an offering unto the Lord" (Moses 5:4–5; emphasis added).

These and many other sacred truths have been restored so that we might understand our relationship as men and women and as children of God. From them we understand, as the psalmist declared, that we are divine—even the "children of the most High" (Psalm 82:6). The scriptural declaration that we were created in the image and likeness of God is the heritage of all who profess to believe in the Bible. Yet the understanding that these words mean what they say is exclusive to Latter-day Saints. We alone profess a God who has body, parts, and passions, a God who is a personal being, one who claims the privilege of being the father of his children. To the words in question, modern revelation adds, "In the image of his own body, male and female, created he them, and blessed them, and called their name Adam" (Moses 6:9). As our children bear our image, so Adam and Eve bore the image of their parents. And Eve, who was to share equally in all the endowments of heaven, also bore the name Adam, thus symbolizing the oneness and unity known to our first mortal parents.

Let us now speak more particularly of the role of the woman as it is unfolded in the revelations of the Restoration. Adam was the "firstborn" of God's children upon the earth (Abraham 1:3). He came, it would appear, to prepare the way for the woman. Of that period in which Adam labored without Eve at his side the Lord said, "It was not good that the man should be alone" (Moses 3:18). The divine plan does not embrace the idea of celibacy, either in this life or in the life to come. It simply is not good for a man to be without a matrimonial companion. The woman, the Lord said, was to be his "help meet"; without her the man has neither the power of creation nor the hope of salvation (see D&C 131:1–4).

All the ordinances of the temple center in the family. Only in the union of the man and the woman is the promise given of thrones, kingdoms, and principalities. Only of those who have entered that sacred covenant is it said, "They shall pass by the angels, and the gods, which are set there, to their exaltation and glory in all things, as hath been sealed upon their heads, which glory shall be a fulness and continuation of the seeds forever and ever. Then shall they be gods, because they have no end; therefore shall they be from everlasting to everlasting, because they continue; then shall they be above all, because all things are subject unto them. Then shall they be gods, because they have all power, and the angels are subject unto them" (D&C 132:19–20).

No bolder declaration could be made, no greater promises extended. The invitation to heirship is extended to his sons and daughters together, but only together, for neither sons nor daughters can obtain it separately or singly. Such principles do not allow for any notion that one gender is of greater importance in the divine plan than another. With the power that is woman's alone, to conceive and give birth to children, has also come a special endowment to love, nurture, and teach their offspring. Men may lay claim to it, but it is not theirs. Because of this, the tradition of near-countless generations has held the place of women to be in the home. Of course this is true. It is equally true that the woman's place is in the temple, and the chapel, and the schools, and the legislative halls, and in all other places where virtue is to be taught and good is to be accomplished. Created in the image and likeness of God, she should be found laboring in all places and all causes that are pleasing to her divine Father. Upon her rests a special endowment to beautify, to bless, to comfort, and to heal. Women were born to teach, to lift, and to encourage; to them alone has been entrusted the power to give life. Where it has been the propensity of men to rule by strength, it has been that of women to change the destiny of nations by the greater power of love.

It is the right of women to dream dreams and to see visions, to entertain angels, and to associate with the Spirit of God. Her counterparts in ages past have declared the truths of salvation, spoken scripture, sung with the voice of angels, and enriched the world with music, art, and the written word. Such is ever her right. We note with reverence that God has not extended to her the right to hold the priesthood, though the fulness of its blessings are hers. We would suppose that a primary reason for that is to respect her role of motherhood and to suggest that no other labor, regardless of how good it may be, should divide her attention from that sacred calling. The restored gospel affirms that nothing in this life or the next will bring greater joy or fulfillment to the woman than that of wife and mother or to the man than that of husband and father.

QUESTION

The doctrine of the Church holds that spiritual gifts and the keys to the mysteries of the kingdom are accessible through the

Melchizedek Priesthood. Are women less eligible than men to exercise spiritual gifts and to comprehend the mysteries of the kingdom?

ANSWER

Spiritual gifts are special talents given by God to his faithful children to strengthen one another and build up his kingdom on earth. These divinely given talents come through the instrumentality of the Holy Ghost. They are the rightful inheritance of all who have had hands laid upon their heads after baptism and have been commanded to receive the Holy Ghost and who have responded positively to that command. The right to possess spiritual gifts is no more a matter of gender than is the right to exercise faith or to repent or to be baptized. It could be argued that because women have a greater propensity for faith and repentance than men they have greater claim on these gifts; but in fairness, it should be said that any who live the law are entitled to its blessings. The laws of heaven are blind to skin color, educational attainments, social status, wealth, gender, age, or any other such distinction. Joseph Smith taught that "there is a law, irrevocably decreed in heaven before the foundations of this world, upon which all blessings are predicated—and when we [and it matters not who "we" are] obtain any blessing from God, it is by obedience to that law upon which it is predicated" (D&C 130:20). Christ invites all to come unto him "and partake of his goodness; and he denieth none that come unto him, black and white, bond and free, male and female; and he remembereth the heathen; and all are alike unto God, both Jew and Gentile" (2 Nephi 26:33). Alma assured us that God "imparteth his word by angels unto men, yea, not only men but women also. Now this is not all; little children do have words given unto them many times, which confound the wise and the learned" (Alma 32:23).

By revelation we are told that the "priesthood administereth the gospel and holdeth the key of the mysteries of the kingdom, even the key of the knowledge of God. Therefore, in the ordinances thereof, the power of godliness is manifest. And without the ordinances thereof, and the authority of the priesthood, the power of godliness is not manifest unto men in the flesh; for without this no man can see the face of God, even the Father, and live" (D&C 84:19–22). Commenting on these verses, some have suggested that holding the priesthood is a requisite to seeing God. That such an interpretation was not intended is evident from the verses that follow: "Now this Moses plainly taught to the children of Israel in the wilderness, and sought diligently to sanctify his people that they might behold the face of God; but they hardened their hearts and could not endure his presence; therefore, the Lord in his wrath, for his anger was kindled against them, swore that they should not enter into his rest while in the wilderness, which rest is the fulness of his glory. Therefore, he took Moses out of their midst, and the Holy Priesthood also" (D&C 84:23–25).

Moses was not seeking to sanctify only the men any more than he intended to lead the men, without their wives and children, into the promised land. All were to be sanctified so that all—men, women, and children—could stand in the presence of their God, and all were to journey together to the land promised them. The story typifies the whole system of salvation and our sojourn in mortality. We make the journey to our land of promise (eternal life) as families. All must be sanctified, for no unclean thing can enter the divine presence. There is no suggestion here that men alone are to be saved or that they alone are to enjoy the blessings of obedience to sacred ordinances. Those blessings take on meaning only as husband and wife stand side by side and then are surrounded by their posterity. When the revelation says, "for without this no man can see the face of God, even the Father, and live" the antecedent of "this" is "the power of godliness," or being sanctified (D&C 84:21–22). The ordinances of the priesthood out of which "the power of godliness" comes bring the same promise of blessings to women that they do to men.

QUESTION

Was it necessary for the Relief Society to be organized before women could receive the temple endowment? Could there be more to Relief Society than most Church members understand?

ANSWER

No. It was not necessary for the Relief Society to be organized before the endowment could be restored. It is the priesthood, not an auxiliary organization, to which we look to find the power to exalt women.

Nonetheless, there is more to Relief Society than most Church members understand. That value centers in its charitable role and in the principles of faith that it teaches, not in some mystical notion that the organization itself somehow rivals or approximates the priesthood. The blessings of salvation are not associated with membership in quorums or auxiliaries. Salvation is in Christ and in our taking upon ourselves his name. That is accomplished in ordinances and in keeping the covenants associated with them. Quorums and auxiliaries exist to help us do that.

QUESTION

If women cannot hold the priesthood, how can they have authority to function in their Church callings? Can they have authority apart from the priesthood? For instance, by what authority do female temple ordinance workers perform ordinances?

ANSWER

The words *priesthood* and *authority*, though often used interchangeably, are not always synonymous. One can hold priesthood and be without authority to do particular things; on the other hand, one can have authority to do particular things and not hold the priesthood. For instance, to preside in one of the Church's auxiliary programs, a person must be properly called, receive the sustaining vote of those over whom he or she presides, and be set apart by the same authority by which he or she was called. In this manner women are given the authority to preside over auxiliary organizations. Now, it might be asked, if their calling is to be an auxiliary to the priesthood, doesn't anyone who holds the priesthood have the authority to direct their efforts? The answer, of course, is no. The Lord's house is a house of order, and such authority is not vested in the priesthood itself. The authority to preside and direct is vested in the keys of the priesthood, which are held exclusively by those in a position of priesthood presidency.

One of the earliest revelations that followed the organization of the Church affirmed that women could properly be called "to expound scriptures, and to exhort the church" under the direction of the Spirit (D&C 25:7). In the temple, women also perform certain ordinances for other women. Those doing so have been given the necessary authority, which is conferred by the laying on of hands by those who have the keys to direct this work.

QUESTION

How do we explain women giving blessings to the sick in Nauvoo?

ANSWER

It is very important to understand the setting in which these blessings took place. In the spring of 1842 the sacred ordinances performed in temples were first revealed by the Prophet Joseph Smith. He spoke with some freedom about these things to the women of the Relief Society, which was organized at this same time. Its leading women would be among the first to receive the ordinances we now associate with the temple. Impressed that something might happen to him before the completion of the temple, the Prophet felt it necessary for the Quorum of the Twelve, their wives, and a few others to receive the blessings of the temple before its completion. This necessitated certain women being given the necessary authority to perform the ordinances of washing and anointing for the sisters. This authority to wash, anoint, and bless as held by the sisters was used in a few instances to administer to the sick. The Prophet had no objection to the sisters using the authority they had been given in this manner. In an address to the newly formed Relief Society, he observed that there "could be no devil in it, if God gave His sanction by healing; that there could be no more sin in any female laying hands on and praying for the sick, than in wetting the face with water; it is no sin for anybody to administer that has faith, or if the sick have faith to be healed by their administration" (*History of the Church,* 4:604). When the temple was completed, however, the use of that authority was restricted to the temple ceremony as performed there (see Dallin H. Oaks, in Conference Report, April 1992, 50).

President Joseph Fielding Smith explained: "The Brethren do not consider it necessary or wise for the women of the Relief Society to wash and anoint women who are sick. The Lord has given us directions in matters of this kind; we are to call in the elders, and they are to anoint with oil on the head and bless by the laying on of hands.

"The Church teaches that a woman may lay on hands upon the head of a sick child and ask the Lord to bless it, in the case when those holding the priesthood cannot be present. A man might under such conditions invite his wife to lay on hands with him in blessing their sick child. This would be merely to exercise her faith and not because of any inherent right to lay on hands. A woman would have no authority to anoint or seal a blessing, and where elders can be called in, that would be the proper way to have an administration performed" (*Doctrines of Salvation,* 3:178).

QUESTION

Why can a man be sealed to more than one wife but a woman can't be sealed to more than one man?

ANSWER

While living, a woman can be sealed to only one man. After her death, she may be sealed to another man if she had also been his wife. The second sealing would require the woman to make a choice about which sealing she would choose to honor in the eternal worlds.

No revealed answer has been given to the question of why a woman cannot have more than one husband at the same time.

QUESTION

How will women who do not marry and have children in mortality spend eternity?

ANSWER

A woman who did not have the opportunity to marry properly but lived worthy of it will have that privilege in the world to come. In like manner, any woman who was denied the privilege of motherhood because of circumstances beyond her control and who lived worthy of it will have that privilege extended to her in the life beyond. The full blessings of motherhood will then be hers. A woman who had no interest in marriage or family in this life will be without the same in the world to come.

QUESTION

How much individual life and personality is a wife and mother "allowed" to have? How can one determine when it is all right to put her own needs first? Or is it never all right?

ANSWER

Every appropriate investment a mother makes in herself reaps dividends in her children. A mother can't teach what she has not taken the time to learn. Expectant mothers are often reminded that they are eating for two. In a spiritual sense, the mother of half a dozen children must fortify her soul to feed six. Perhaps the rule of thumb is that the greater the difficulty a mother has in finding time for proper rest, refreshment, and spiritual renewal, the greater the need for them and the greater the dividends in the lives of her children. Significantly, those days in which we don't have time for prayer are the days in which we have the greatest need for prayer. Similarly, those days in which there is no time to eat or rest or find a brief spiritual respite are the days in which those things are most needed. These are matters on which the needs of the mother must come first, simply because even the best mothers cannot share what they do not possess.

QUESTION

Is it better for a woman to remain single all her life than to marry outside the Church?

ANSWER

The question itself is lopsided. It is like asking, Is it better to work on Sunday, or starve to death? Of course we don't want anyone to starve to death, but does that mean if a person passes up a particular job offer, he or she will starve? Frankly, it is doubtful. This question assumes that if a woman refuses a particular proposal, no others will come and of necessity she will be lonely. Let's not kid ourselves: to accept a second-rate marriage proposal is a pretty good way to assure that a woman is going to be lonely (if not in this life, then certainly in the next, and there is a good probability that she will be lonely in both). The assumption that no other proposals will come hardly radiates faith. What needs to be recaptured here is the idea that God blesses those who exercise faith.

It is hard to suppose that someone with a meaningful understanding of the gospel would marry outside the faith. Those who have done so have often found that their posterity also end up out of the Church.

AT ISSUE

At issue is the proper place of women in the Church and kingdom of God. Given that the whole system of salvation centers in the eternal union of the man and the woman and that salvation is indeed a family affair, one can hardly overstate the place of women. Having created both the man and the woman in his image and likeness and having sealed them as man and wife, God "called their name Adam" (Moses 6:9), symbolizing the unity and oneness that was to exist between them.

The proper place of women is always lost in times of apostasy. Of this we can be perfectly sure—it will never be found by looking to or imitating the standards of the world. Only in the restored gospel do we find a corporeal resurrection—one that preserves gender distinctions in order that husbands and wives may continue in their respective roles of life-giver through the endless eternities. Only in the restored gospel do we speak of the man and the woman inheriting together "thrones, kingdoms, principalities, and powers, dominions, all heights and depths" (D&C 132:19). Only in the restored gospel are the man and the woman sealed together that they might receive the fulness of their divine Father. "Therefore," the word of God declares, "shall they [the man and the woman] be from everlasting to everlasting, because they continue; then shall they be above all, because all things are subject unto them. Then shall they be gods, because they have all power, and the angels are subject unto them" (D&C 132:20). Any fashion, style, philosophy, or movement that does not lead to this end is not of God nor does it have a proper place among his people.

CHAPTER NINE

SCIENCE AND RELIGION

How old is the earth?

How do you square the revelation that states that the earth has only seven thousand years of temporal existence with the dictums of science that tell us that things have been living and dying far longer than that?

Is the theory of evolution compatible with the doctrine of the Fall?

What do the revelations of the Restoration teach us about the origin of man and the creation of the earth that go beyond the biblical account?

Did God discover law, or is he the author of it?

If God is the author of all law, does that mean that he can do whatever he wants?

Can God do all things?

Could God cease to be God?

How did God become God?

Is a mastery of the laws of mathematics and science necessary to the process of obtaining exaltation?

A S A PEOPLE WE HAVE OFTEN taken pains to assure the rising generation that there is no conflict between "true" science and "true" religion. Properly understood, we have repeatedly been told, both will always be in harmony. The difficulty with such a statement is that it makes neither good science nor good religion. Science, as it is generally understood, is decidedly neutral on all matters of interest to religion. Science knows neither justice nor mercy, good nor evil, right nor wrong. It claims neither the power to remit sins nor the authority to identify them. It knows nothing of faith, repentance, redemption, or life beyond the grave. It demands neither ritual nor righteousness. Religion, on the other hand, knows no neutrality. Individuals accept or reject true religion at the peril of their eternal life. Religion, which is a bond between God and man, professes to embrace both mercy and justice and to define both good and evil. The laws of science reject the notion of a resurrection, the inseparable union of body and spirit; religion claims God to be the source of both immortality and eternal life. The dogmas of science are in constant flux; the verities of religion remain everlastingly the same. Science favors no one cause over another; religion professes to bless the faithful and condemn the faithless.

Science is inherently neither antagonistic to religion nor supportive of it. It is simply a tool, a way to search for understanding and knowledge in a temporal world. Some use science to build faith, others to oppose it, and still others as a substitute for it. The decision of how it is to be used rests with those using it. Some scientists are men of faith; others are not. Those seeking confirmation of religious truths generally find it; those seeking to disprove spiritual truths enjoy equal success.

Using the scientific method we seek to understand the physical universe of which we are a part. It has proved itself a fit tool for doing so. It is not effective, however, in finding spiritual truths. If we would know the things of the Spirit, we must become conversant with the laws that govern spiritual things. The laws of science respond with the same consistency for evil men and their purposes as they do for the noble and righteous; but the powers of heaven are inseparably connected with righteousness (see D&C

121:36). "There is a law, irrevocably decreed in heaven before the foundations of this world, upon which all blessings are predicated—and when we obtain any blessing from God, it is by obedience to that law upon which it is predicated" (D&C 130:20–21). God is not subservient to the laws of the physical universe. Indeed, he created them. Thus he can answer prayers faster than the speed of light. The laws that govern in the celestial realm are far beyond those known to us in this temporal, telestial state in which we find ourselves.

QUESTION

How old is the earth?

ANSWER

It's difficult to say how old the earth is, but the question has little relevance to understanding the creation process. From the time God completed the creation of the earth and pronounced it "very good" (Moses 2:31) to the time that Adam and Eve partook of the forbidden fruit and introduced the Fall, time was not measured as it is now. In that Edenic state, there was no aging or decay: all things simply remained in the state they were in after they were created (see 2 Nephi 2:22; Moses 3:9). How can we measure that which does not exist?

The scriptures do tell us that God created the world in six days and rested on the seventh. It would be hard to argue that these were six days of twenty-four hours, given that it was not until the fourth day of creation that God created the sun and the moon and divided the day from the night (see Genesis 1:14–19; Moses 2:14–19). In fact, the account in Abraham speaks of the creative periods as times rather than as days (see Abraham 4:8, 13, 19, 23, 31; 5:2–3). It may be that the days of creation each consisted of whatever time was necessary to accomplish the assigned task, and when it was completed, that was "a day." Thus the term *day* is used to designate an unspecified period of time, as in the "day of afflic-tion," the "day of probation," the "day of deliverance," the "day of visitation," and so forth.

In measures of time known to man, we do not know how long it took to create the earth or how long Adam and Eve chose to remain in their Edenic state. The revelations do specifically tell us the period of time during which the earth will be subject to the effects of Adam's fall, that is, death, decay, and corruption. This earth, the Prophet Joseph Smith was told, will have "seven thou-sand years of . . . continuance, or . . . temporal existence" (D&C 77:6; see also v. 12). A "temporal existence" is one in which there is death, one in which things are other than eternal.

QUESTION

How do you square the revelation that states that the earth has only seven thousand years of temporal existence with the dictums of science that tell us that things have been living and dying far longer than that?

ANSWER

The first issue here is whether we square the revelations of God with the theories of men, or test the theories of men against the revelations. That has a great deal to do with the kind of con-clusion we come to. If we try to square religion with science, and this has been done plenty of times, we simply say that the language of the revelation doesn't mean what it says it means. On the other hand, if we are squaring science with revelation, we conclude that there hasn't been death on this earth as long as the theories of men tell us there has.

How does Latter-day Saint theology respond to the discrep-ancy between science and religion about the time period in which there has been both life and death on the earth? Neither the scrip-tures nor the prophets have felt any particular need to respond to this matter. We are trusted to find answers to such questions on our own. In that process some have done better than others. Of particular importance in seeking to resolve this issue is the assumption underlying the conclusions of science that all life forms evolved on the earth and that conditions have been essentially uniform. Our theology rejects both assumptions outright. By revelation we have been told that all things were created spiritually first and thus all life forms came from another sphere (see Moses 3:5). Further, the newly created earth was governed by an Edenic, or paradisiacal, law, that is, a law that would equate with a terrestrial order. By contrast, our present earth is governed by telestial law, which is vastly different. For a theologian the question is, How can data gathered on a telestial earth answer questions about existence on a terrestrial earth? We do not study grapes to draw conclusions about pumpkins, nor do we study the moon to learn about life forms on the sun. Why then would we study a telestial earth to draw conclusions about creation in a terrestrial world?

It might also be observed that priesthood powers are not circumscribed by natural law. By the authority of the priesthood, water can be turned into vintage wine in an instant. Yet experts claim that years are necessary. Again, contrary to the observable and documentable laws of nature, broken bones can be healed instantly, and those who have been dead for thousands of years can come forth to reclaim their bodies in a state of immortality. Such happenings do not make good science, but they make marvelous religion.

QUESTION

Is the theory of evolution compatible with the doctrine of the Fall?

ANSWER

No. We can tug, twist, contort, and sell our birthright, but we cannot overcome the irreconcilable differences between the theory of organic evolution and the doctrine of the Fall. Some have argued for a form of theistic evolution—that is, a God-inspired evolution—in which lower forms of life progressed over great periods of time to the point that God could take the spirit of the man Adam and place it in an animal and declare it to be the first man. The argument is at odds both with scripture and with an official declaration of the First Presidency on the origin of man. The scriptures of the Restoration declare Adam to be "the son of God" (Moses 6:22) and the "firstborn" of all earth's inhabitants (Abraham 1:3). They further state that he and Eve were created in the image and likeness of God's body. In the book of Moses we read: "In the day that God created man, in the likeness of God made he him; *in the image of his own body*, male and female, created he them, and blessed them, and called their name Adam, in the day when they were created and became living souls in the land upon the footstool of God" (Moses 6:8–9; emphasis added). Let the idea not be lost that the physical body of God is being spoken of here. This plain declaration is sustained by the Book of Mormon, which teaches that the premortal Christ would take upon himself "the image of man, and it should be the *image after which man was created in the beginning*; or in other words, he said that man was created after the image of God, and that God should come down among the children of men, and take upon him flesh and blood, and go forth upon the face of the earth" (Mosiah 7:27; emphasis added). Similarly, the official statement of the First Presidency is that "Adam, our progenitor, 'the first man,' was, like Christ, a pre-existent spirit, and like Christ he took upon him an appropriate body, the body of a man, and so became a 'living soul.' The doctrine of the pre-existence,—revealed so plainly, particularly in latter days, pours a wonderful flood of light upon the otherwise mysterious problem of man's origin. It shows that man, as a spirit, was begotten and born of heavenly parents, and reared to maturity in the eternal mansions of the Father, prior to coming upon the earth in a temporal body to undergo an experience in mortality. It teaches that all men existed in the spirit before any man existed in the flesh, *and that all who have inhabited the earth since Adam have taken bodies and become souls in like manner"* (Clark, *Messages of the First Presidency,* 4:205; emphasis added). Be it Adam, Christ, or any other human being, the process of birth is the same. The First Presidency continues, "Man is the child of God, formed in the divine image and endowed with divine attributes" (ibid., 4:206).

Evolution is the notion that lower forms of life can, through the course of generations, genetically improve themselves. For that to happen, both birth and death would have to exist. By contrast, Father Lehi teaches us that if there had been no Fall, "all things which were created must have remained in the same state in which they were after they were created; and they must have remained forever, and had no end. And they would have had no children," he tells us. Thus, he testifies, "Adam fell that men might be" (2 Nephi 2:22–23, 25). Enoch, teaching the same thing, said: "Because that Adam fell, we are; and by his fall came death; and we are made partakers of misery and woe" (Moses 6:48).

The gospel of Jesus Christ rests on the union of three doctrines—the Creation, the Fall, and the Atonement. They have been aptly called the three pillars of eternity. No meaningful understanding of the gospel can be had independent of an understanding of the interrelationship of these three doctrines. Unless we understand how things were created—that is, the original state or nature of things in prefallen earth—we cannot understand what they fell from or what the redemption seeks to return them to. Latter-day Saint theology recognizes God as the Creator. Thus the labor of creation must be godlike. God does not do shoddy work. Having completed the work of creation, he declared it "very good" (Moses 2:31). All created things were in a paradisiacal state—a state in which there was no corruption, no aging, decay, pain, sickness, or death. It is this state to which the atonement of Christ seeks to return us, and it was from this state that Adam fell. This is a matter of devolving, not evolving. Well might we ask, Did Christ redeem us from our present condition to take us back to a more primitive one, one in which living organisms are fighting with and destroying each other? We could hardly consider that a state of glory, yet the promise of the scriptures is that the earth is to be renewed and receive again "its paradisiacal glory" (Article of Faith 10).

Some have argued that the paradisiacal glory of which we speak was confined to the Garden of Eden while evolutionary processes were taking place through the rest of the earth. The great difficulty with this idea is that it confines the effects of the Atonement to forty acres (or whatever size the Garden of Eden was). The plain testimony of scripture is that the entire earth and all created things were affected by the Fall and thus recipients of the blessings of the Atonement. "Every corruptible thing, both of man, or of the beasts of the field, or of the fowls of the heavens, or of the fish of the sea, that dwells upon all the face of the earth, shall be consumed" when the earth makes its transition back to its Edenic state. At that time "all things shall become new," and the "knowledge and glory" of God will fill the earth (D&C 101:24–25). "And in that day the enmity of man, and the enmity of beasts, yea, the enmity of all flesh, shall cease," and there will be "no death," for individuals will, at the appropriate time, be "changed in the twinkling of an eye, and shall be caught up" to an even more glorious rest (D&C 101:26, 29, 31).

Elder Boyd K. Packer observed that if the theory of evolution applies to man, there was no fall and therefore no need for an atonement, nor a gospel of redemption, nor a redeemer (see "The Law and the Light," 15). The matter is really quite simple. Because Adam was the son of divine parents, he had an immortal body without blood. The Fall caused blood to enter his veins. It was a blood fall that required a blood atonement. One cannot tamper with the story of the Fall without tampering with the story of the

Atonement. If it was not Adam who introduced blood and its companion death through his transgression, then we had better find out who did and when it happened so that the necessary corrections can be made in the plan of salvation.

In a further attempt to harmonize evolution with the gospel, some have separated man from the evolutionary process. They concede that man is the creation of God but maintain that the earth and all other life forms were created by evolution. Yet we know that all life forms were represented in Eden and like Adam and Eve were subjects of the Fall. Because of Adam they too will die and because of Christ they too will have claim upon immortality and eternal life. On the matter of the resurrection of animals Joseph Smith said: "Any man who would tell you that this could not be, would tell you the revelations are not true" (*Teachings of the Prophet Joseph Smith*, 291). To argue for the existence of life forms that were not subject to Adam's fall is to argue at the same time that they are not redeemed through Christ's atonement. Such an argument places God in the awkward position of creating that which he does not have the power to save.

QUESTION

What do the revelations of the Restoration teach us about the origin of man and the creation of the earth that go beyond the biblical account?

ANSWER

Speaking of what we learn in the revelations of the Restoration about the origin of man, the First Presidency has used the expression "a wonderful flood of light" ("Origin of Man," 80). Consider the following:

The elements are eternal. The traditional Christian world holds the doctrine of creation ex nihilo, meaning creation out of nothing. Joseph Smith announced to us that "the elements are eternal" (D&C 93:33) and explained that "there is no such thing as immaterial matter. All spirit is matter, but it is more fine or pure, and can only be discerned by purer eyes; we cannot see it; but when our bodies are purified we shall see that it is all matter" (D&C 131:7–8). Exploring the meaning of the Hebrew word translated "create" in the book of Genesis, Joseph Smith told us that that word "does not mean to create out of nothing; it means to organize; the same as a man would organize materials and build a ship. Hence, we infer that God had materials to organize the world out of chaos—chaotic matter, which is element, and in which dwells all the glory. Elements had an existence from the time he had. The pure principles of element are principles which can never be destroyed; they may be organized and re-organized, but not destroyed. They had no beginning, and can have no end" (*Teachings of the Prophet Joseph Smith*, 350–52).

The notion that man was created out of nothing is a hallmark of the Apostasy. Such a notion sustains the idea that God has neither body nor parts and that he is our Father and we are his children only in a figurative sense. The effect of such a doctrine is to distance us from God and from an understanding of his nature. The view you have of the Creation reflects the view you have of the Creator. How are we to feel close to a formless essence that created us from nothing? By contrast, we naturally feel close to a loving Father who created us from his own bone and sinew and who once embraced us.

"I made the world, and men before they were in the flesh," the Lord declared (Moses 6:51). All living things were born first as spirits and then took upon them a physical tabernacle. Having recounted the story of creation, the book of Moses explains how things took place: "For I, the Lord God, created all things, of which I have spoken, spiritually, before they were naturally upon the face of the earth," we are told. "In heaven created I them; and there was not yet flesh upon the earth, neither in the water, neither in the air" (Moses 3:5). This means that all life forms existed first in a spirit realm where they were schooled and trained for the experiences of mortality. Thus we understand why we call God our Father in Heaven. He was literally that, the Father of our spirits, and when we read that we were created in his image and likeness, we know it to be literally so. As it is with man, so it is with all things. "That which is spiritual being in the likeness of that which is temporal; and that which is temporal in the likeness of that which is spiritual; the spirit of man in the likeness of his person, as also the spirit of the beast, and every other creature which God has created" (D&C 77:2).

Spirit children of our Father were involved in the creation of the earth. We first learn this doctrine in the book of Abraham. Here we are told that from among the noble and great ones were those who sat in council to lay the plans for the creation of this earth. Of these the text says, "We will go down, for there is space there, and we will take of these materials, and we will make an earth whereon these [their kindred spirits] may dwell" (Abraham 3:24). At the conclusion of that great council, those thus involved, who were called Gods, said, "We will do everything that we have said, and organize them; and behold, they shall be very obedient." And so it was that "they went down at the beginning, and they, that is the Gods, organized and formed the heavens and the earth" (Abraham 4:31, 1).

As first created in their physical form, no living thing was subject to death. Consider what we are taught in Moses 3:7. This passage announces that God created "man from the dust of the ground," a metaphor for the normal birth process and understood as such by prophets in both the Old and New Worlds. Enoch, for example, used this metaphor in the same manner as Moses did (see Moses 6:59), and Jacob said, "All flesh is of the dust" (Jacob 2:21). Similarly, speaking to his people, King Benjamin said, "Ye were created of the dust of the earth" (Mosiah 2:25), and Moroni said, "Man was created of the dust of the earth" (Mormon 9:17).

Moses 3:7 then tells us that God "breathed into his nostrils the breath of life; and man became a living soul." Again the reference is to "the spirit and the body" (D&C 88:15). Continuing, the text declares, "The first flesh upon the earth, the first man also" (Moses 3:7). *Flesh* means mortality (see LDS Bible Dictionary, 675); thus we understand that Adam was both the first of all of God's creations to be subject to death—he having introduced death by partaking of the fruit—and that there were no pre-Adamites, because he was the "first man." "Nevertheless, all things were before created [that is, as spirits]; but spiritually were they created and made according to my word" (Moses 3:7). In this passage the word "spiritually" means that which is not subject to death. All the revelations of the Restoration use the word in this manner (see Alma 11:45; D&C 88:27–28).

This world will know seven thousand years of temporal history (see also pages 156–57). Doctrine and Covenants 88, our great revelation on resurrection, delineates the seven angels who will sound their trump, each calling for the revelation of the secret acts of men during each of the seven thousand years of the earth's temporal history. To argue for a longer time is to suggest ages for which God has forgotten to call for accountability (see D&C 88:108–10).

"In the beginning of the seventh thousand years will the Lord God sanctify the earth, and complete the salvation of man" (D&C 77:12). This transition will embrace all corruptible things, including man, beasts of the field, fowls of the heavens, and fish of the sea, and was described even in ancient revelation as a new heaven and a new earth (see D&C 101:24; Isaiah 65:17). That all forms of life are subject to the affects of the Fall and thus are rightful heirs of the blessings of Christ's redemption affirms that they, like man, are not the product of an evolutionary process.

At the end of the Millennium the earth and all that inhabit it will be changed from a paradisiacal, or terrestrial, state to a celestial state. The earth, the revelations tell us, is a living thing, which means that it too was among those things that were created as a spirit before it was clothed in a physical tabernacle. Thus it will yet die, be resurrected, obtain a celestial glory, and become the home of all who once resided on it who also obtain that glory (see D&C 88:25–26). Describing the transition from its paradisiacal to its exalted state, the Lord said: "The end shall come, and the heaven and the earth shall be consumed and pass away, and there shall be a new heaven and a new earth. For all old things shall pass away, and all things shall become new, even the heaven and the earth, and all the fulness thereof, both men and beasts, the fowls of the air, and the fishes of the sea; and not one hair, neither mote [small particle], shall be lost, for it is the workmanship of mine hand" (D&C 29:23–25). After inquiring what the "sea of glass" was spoken of by John the Revelator in Revelation 4:6, Joseph Smith was told: "It is the earth, in its sanctified, immortal, and eternal state" (D&C 77:1). He was further told that "this earth, in its sanctified and immortal state, will be made like unto crystal and will be a Urim and Thummim to the inhabitants who dwell thereon, whereby all things pertaining to an inferior kingdom, or all kingdoms of a lower order, will be manifest to those who dwell on it; and this earth will be Christ's" (D&C 130:9).

QUESTION

Did God discover law, or is he the author of it?

ANSWER

God is the author of law, not its creation or its servant. All light and all law emanate from him (see D&C 88:13). Indeed, "all kingdoms have a law given; and there are many kingdoms; for there is no space in the which there is no kingdom; and there is no kingdom in which there is no space, either a greater or a lesser kingdom. And unto every kingdom is given a law; and unto every law there are certain bounds also and conditions" (D&C 88:36–38). Of God the revelation states, "He comprehendeth all things, and all things are before him, and all things are round about him; and he is above all things, and in all things, and is through all things, and is round about all things; and all things are by him, and of him, even God, forever and ever" (D&C 88:41).

Joseph Smith asked, "Can we suppose that He [God] has a kingdom without laws? Or do we believe that it is composed of an innumerable company of beings who are entirely beyond all law? Consequently have need of nothing to govern or regulate them? Would not such ideas be a reproach to our Great Parent, and at variance with His glorious intelligence? Would it not be asserting that man had found out a secret beyond Deity? That he had learned that it was good to have laws, while God after existing from eternity and having power to create man, had not found out that it was proper to have laws for His government?" (*Teachings of the Prophet Joseph Smith*, 55).

"God," Joseph Smith taught, "has made certain decrees which are fixed and immovable; for instance, God set the sun, the moon, and the stars in the heavens, and gave them their laws, conditions and bounds, which they cannot pass, except by His commandments; they all move in perfect harmony in their sphere and order, and are as lights, wonders and signs unto us. The sea also has its bounds which it cannot pass. God has set many signs on the earth, as well as in the heavens; for instance, the oak of the forest, the fruit of the tree, the herb of the field, all bear a sign that seed hath been planted there; for it is a decree of the Lord that every tree, plant, and herb bearing seed should bring forth of its kind, and cannot come forth after any other law or principle" (*Teachings of the Prophet Joseph Smith*, 197–98).

God is not a scientist. He does not harness law and then use it to bless and govern his creations. God is the author and source of all law. Were this not the case, the powers of evil could seek his overthrow through the discovery of unknown laws. We would live in endless peril. Our prayers would then be *for* God, not *to* him, and scientists rather than prophets would hold the keys of salvation.

167

True it is that God was once a man obtaining his exalted status by obedience to the laws of his own eternal Father, but upon obtaining that station he becomes the source of light and law to all that he creates. Following this same pattern, the resurrected Christ said to the Nephites, "I am the law" (3 Nephi 15:9).

QUESTION

If God is the author of all law, does that mean that he can do whatever he wants?

ANSWER

The question seems to imply that if God were not bound by law, we are not sure he could be trusted. How can we exercise faith in a God who can't be trusted? By definition a God does only that which is godly. Teaching this principle, Joseph Smith said, "Whatever God requires is right, no matter what it is, although we may not see the reason thereof till long after the events transpire" (*Teachings of the Prophet Joseph Smith*, 256).

QUESTION

Can God do all things?

ANSWER

This is the kind of question asked in an attempt to embarrass or confuse someone. If an affirmative response is given, the trap is sprung with a second question, Can he make a stone so big he cannot move it? In other words, can God do that which he cannot do? We avoid the silliness of such discussions with the understanding that notwithstanding that God has all knowledge and all understanding, there are many things he cannot do. He cannot do that which is ungodly. He cannot lack wisdom, knowledge, or virtue. He cannot be evil, mean, or petty. He cannot exalt or save the unrepentant. He cannot do anything that is not in the best interest of his children.

QUESTION

Could God cease to be God?

ANSWER

No. As a dramatic teaching device someone might say, If God ceased to do such and such (citing any attribute or action that is godly), he would cease to be God. This is simply a way of dramatizing that God is never derelict in his duty, he does not have off days, his word is sure. We exercise faith in him because of the perfection of his attributes and because of their constancy. God does not slip, he does not make mistakes, and he is in no danger of apostatizing. He cannot be impeached or dethroned. He does not grow old and cannot die. God simply cannot cease to be God.

QUESTION

How did God become God?

ANSWER

Joseph Smith said, "God himself was once as we are now, and is an exalted man, and sits enthroned in yonder heavens!" (*Teachings of the Prophet Joseph Smith,* 345). He obtained his exaltation by following the same path that he has marked for us. Thus our revelations tell us that a man and his wife may receive the promise, in the house of the Lord, that they will come forth in the first resurrection and inherit "thrones, kingdoms, principalities, and powers, dominions, all heights and depths" (D&C 132:19). Of those who obtain this status the revelation states: "Then shall they be gods, because they have no end; therefore shall they be from everlasting to everlasting, because they continue; then shall they be above all, because all things are subject unto them. Then shall they be gods, because they have all power, and the angels are subject unto them" (D&C 132:20). If we as the children of God can obtain "all power" and have "all things" subject to us, there can be no question about God having that power.

Christ is the perfect example of what is involved in obtaining exaltation. He advanced from grace to grace until he received a fulness of the glory of the Father, and thus enjoyed all power in heaven and on earth (see D&C 93:11–20). Such is the path that we too are to follow.

QUESTION

Is a mastery of the laws of mathematics and science necessary to the process of obtaining exaltation?

ANSWER

If they are, we are yet to receive the revelation that tells us so. Rather, the revelations state that "to him who overcometh, and keepeth my commandments unto the end, will I give power over many kingdoms; and he shall rule them with the word of God; and they shall be in his hands as the vessels of clay in the hands of a potter; and he shall govern them by faith, with equity and justice, even as I received of my Father" (JST Revelation 2:26–27).

Many passages of scripture exalt learning: "The glory of God is intelligence" (D&C 93:36). "It is impossible for a man to be saved in ignorance" (D&C 131:6). "If a person gains more knowledge and intelligence in this life through his diligence and obedience than another, he will have so much the advantage in the world to come" (D&C 130:19).

Properly understood, such texts center our attention on things of the spirit rather than the intellect. It is not to the learning of the classroom to which these passages of scripture refer but rather to those things that can only be learned in the service of others. It is good doctrine to say that "the glory of God is intelligence" if it is understood that the "intelligence" being described is "light and truth" which can be obtained only by forsaking the "evil one" and, conversely, is lost by "disobedience" and an allegiance to the "tradition of their fathers" or the learning of men (D&C 93:36–39). Similarly, the revelation states that we cannot be saved in ignorance, meaning that we cannot be saved in ignorance of the saving principles of the gospel of Jesus Christ, or more particularly to the revelation, our calling and election must have been made sure (see D&C 131:5–6). Again, the word of the Lord that whatever degree of intelligence we obtain in this life will be so much to our advantage in the world to come refers to that knowledge obtained by "diligence" and "obedience" to the laws and ordinances of the gospel, not to book learning.

With the exception of false theories and practices, nothing in such declarations is intended to demean the learning that comes from schools. Rather, their purpose is to help us focus on the learning of greatest worth (learning that can often be enhanced by the understanding that comes from the study of such things as mathematics and science). Of importance here is the idea that schooling is not a requisite for baptism, whereas faith and repentance are, and that our mentors in obtaining the knowledge of most worth are apostles and prophets, not college professors or those learned in the things of the world.

AT ISSUE

Great effort has been expended to find and sustain harmony between science and religion. Such efforts are born of an allegiance to science, not faith in Christ. They are a way of saying that if something can be demonstrated by science, we can safely exercise faith in it. Thus we find doctrines or principles that cannot be sustained by the laws of science being brought into accord with them.

In fact, true science and true religion are incompatible by their very definition. Science centers in demonstrable facts; true religion centers in faith in the unseen. The laws of science cannot be used to sustain existence of a personal God. Precious few scientists believe in such a God, and those who do, do so as men of faith, not as scientists. The great doctrines of our faith are not scientifically defensible. We cannot prove the doctrine of a corporeal resurrection with scientific principles. Science does not admit to the possibility of immortality. Science does not attempt to prove the fatherhood of God or that in a future state we may be equal with him in power, might, and dominion. Science provides no evidence that Jesus of Nazareth was literally the Son of God and that in and through his atoning sacrifice we may obtain victory over all the effects of Adam's fall. Indeed, it does not sustain the idea that there ever was an Adam or that he and all of God's creations fell from a higher state to the world of corruption in which we now live. Surely we should give thanks to God for the countless blessings that come to us through science, but we should not confuse those blessings with the plan of salvation.

Also at issue is the inseparable relationship among the doctrines of the Creation, the Fall, and the Atonement. A proper understanding of the Creation is essential to an understanding of the Fall, which in turn is essential to a proper understanding of the Atonement. One cannot truly understand any of these principles without a correct understanding of the others.

CHAPTER TEN

QUESTIONS COMMON TO THOSE WHO QUESTION

Isn't the profession of faith simply a crutch for those who have a need to believe?

Aren't there a lot of people in testimony meetings professing to know the Church is true who really only hope or believe the Church to be true?

Are all callings in the Church made by inspiration?

Why can General Authorities disagree on doctrinal matters?

How can prophets be deceived, as in the case of Mark Hoffman?

If we can't trust the judgment of the prophet in everything, how can we trust it in anything?

Isn't it racist or chauvinistic to believe that we are a chosen people?

Is it logical to suppose that we are literally Abraham's seed? Isn't this really figurative?

Do patriarchs declare lineage or assign it?

What of those who are adopted into the house of Israel? Is there an actual change in their blood so that they and their posterity become literal descendants of Abraham?

Why did God give Adam and Eve conflicting commandments in the
Garden of Eden?
Why did King Benjamin say that "the natural man is an enemy to God"?
(Mosiah 3:19). We are children of our Father in Heaven, so shouldn't
our natural tendencies be toward goodness?
In Alma 32 we learn that when we have knowledge, our faith becomes
dormant. If God has all knowledge, as the scriptures tell us, can he have
faith?
What do you do when you receive no answer to your prayers?

WE HAVE NO OBLIGATION TO respond to every objection raised
about our faith. President Ezra Taft Benson explained: "Our
main task is to declare the gospel and do it effectively. We are not
obligated to answer every objection. Every man eventually is
backed up to the wall of faith, and there he must make his stand"
(*Teachings of Ezra Taft Benson*, 206). Everyone has unanswered
questions, and no one gets all the answers in this life. To do so
would defeat the purpose of our mortal probation, for it is a time
of testing, and the test is of faith. Our revelations declare that only
those "who overcome by faith" can inherit the celestial kingdom
(D&C 76:53).

We are all responsible for our own choices, including our
choice of what we will believe and what we will not believe. By
revelation we are directed to seek learning even by faith (see D&C
88:118). The eyes of faith enable us to see much that otherwise
goes unobserved, whereas those who refuse to see and feel the
things of the Spirit eventually become blind to such things and
beyond feeling (see Alma 12:9–11; 1 Nephi 17:45). That is the
reason that the scriptures warn so frequently of those who have
eyes to see and see not and ears to hear and hear not (see Isaiah
6:10; Jeremiah 5:21; Ezekiel 12:2; Matthew 13:15–16; D&C
136:32).

Accordingly, some of our questions will remain unanswered (at
least for a time and season); on the other hand we have the

promise of "wisdom and great treasures of knowledge, even hidden treasures" (D&C 89:19). In sharing those treasures, we are cautioned to "give not that which is holy unto the dogs, neither cast ye your pearls before swine, lest they trample them under their feet, and turn again and rend you" (Matthew 7:6). The divine injunction is to treasure up in our minds "continually the words of life," with the promise that we will be given to know "that portion that shall be meted unto every man" (D&C 84:85). Thus, all who seek after truth will be granted all that they are prepared to receive.

QUESTION

Isn't the profession of faith simply a crutch for those who have a need to believe?

ANSWER

Quite the contrary. In truth, the refusal to believe is a crutch used by those who do not want to assume the responsibility associated with accepting gospel truths. Amulek provides a good illustration. "I did harden my heart," he said, "for I was called many times and I would not hear; therefore I knew concerning these things, yet I would not know; therefore I went on rebelling against God, in the wickedness of my heart" (Alma 10:6).

We are all born into this life with certain spiritual instincts. Chief among them is the ability to know the verity of gospel truths when we hear them. "Faith cometh by hearing, and hearing by the word of God," taught the apostle Paul (Romans 10:17). That testimony, Joseph Smith said, is "always attended by the Spirit of prophecy and revelation" (*Teachings of the Prophet Joseph Smith,* 148). "Truth carries its own influence and recommends itself," the Prophet said (Ehat and Cook, *Words of Joseph Smith,* 237; spelling standardized).

There is no shortage of people who know the message of our

missionaries is true but who refuse to acknowledge its truthfulness because they would then be obligated to act upon that knowledge. As long as they can pretend to be uncertain about the truthfulness of the gospel, they can justify themselves in failing to conform to its standards. Speaking of such people, the Lord said: "They desire to know the truth in part, but not all, for they are not right before me and must needs repent" (D&C 49:2).

QUESTION

Aren't there a lot of people in testimony meetings professing to know the Church is true who really only hope or believe the Church to be true?

ANSWER

A testimony, or knowledge, of the truthfulness of the gospel is something with which we were born. We all knew that the gospel was true long before we entered our present mortal state. Our inability to describe the understanding and feelings that are ours does not argue against their existence. None of us knows gospel truths as well as we ought to, and none of us is as articulate in sharing our feelings with others as we would like to be. The important thing is that testimonies are always strengthened through our efforts to share them. In bearing our testimony we may surprise ourselves with the positiveness of the assertions we make. It should be remembered that when we speak of things of the Spirit, we are entitled to the companionship of the Holy Ghost, and the Holy Ghost is positive, not negative. We cannot have the Spirit as our companion and at the same time lack confidence in what we are saying.

QUESTION

Are all callings in the Church made by inspiration?

ANSWER

The Church is governed through the Spirit of revelation, and callings are extended by that same Spirit. To suppose there are no exceptions to this principle, however, is to suppose that we have no inexperienced leaders or that none of us has ever been distracted by influences contrary to the Spirit. The greater question is, Will the Lord sustain any man or woman in any office and calling that may come to them if they endeavor to serve to the best of their ability? Of that there is no question. The person called becomes the Lord's anointed, and even if the Lord would have preferred someone else, the one called is entitled to inspiration. If such individuals seek to magnify their calling, they will succeed in the assignment given them and be blessed by their service, and we will be blessed by sustaining them.

QUESTION

Why can General Authorities disagree on doctrinal matters?

ANSWER

It comes as a matter of surprise to many people that Church leaders do not always have the same understanding of all gospel principles. That surprise reflects the confidence the members have in their leaders and suggests that they almost expect the leaders to be infallible. It also suggests that they equate priesthood offices with knowledge. It would be comfortable to suppose that among our leaders there are no unanswered questions and that a perfect equality of understanding exists. Realizing that each of us is responsible for our own understanding and that no two people are at exactly the same place in that process is an important lesson. It is also important to realize that we cannot always lean on others. To walk by borrowed light is necessary for a time and a season, but at some point it is expected that we take our place as the source of light for others.

There is room in the Church for differences of understanding. On matters about which the revelations are plain, however, there ought to be a unity of thought and faith. We need not put question marks at the end of revealed pronouncements. We sustain the man who stands at the head of the Church as the living constitution of the Church. We follow the direction he points and accept his voice as final where doctrinal differences may exist. Such authority must rest with him if the Lord's house is to be a house of order and if we are to avoid being tossed about by every wind of doctrine. This is simply to say that there is but one head, and in this sense, one spokesman, for the Church.

It is not to be expected, however, that every General Authority will be the equal of every other General Authority in doctrinal understanding any more than it is to be expected that every bishop have the same understanding as every other bishop or every Sunday School teacher have the same understanding as every other Sunday School teacher. It is common to see people change and improve their views in the process of serving. We should all find ourselves giving better answers to questions and preaching better doctrine with the passing of years. That is true at all levels of the Church. It is also to be expected that the present generation can and will improve upon the preceding generation. Surely we are obligated to improve upon what we have been given. There is danger that some may use that idea as justification to liberalize their views and move further and further from the mainstream of faith and truth. That is a shabby counterfeit to be guarded against. The greater danger rests in our refusing to move forward, announcing that what we have received is sufficient and that nothing more can be added to it. Warning against such an attitude the Lord said: "From them that shall say, We have enough, from them shall be taken away even that which they have" (2 Nephi 28:30).

Thus, in those instances when the views of one man reach beyond those of another, we ought to rejoice in the additional knowledge and in the realization that the process of spiritual growth is alive and well in the Church. To do so will require that we surrender our security blanket (or the notion that in this mortal world all are equal in understanding) and realize that learning the gospel is a process, not an office, and that each individual is responsible for what he or she chooses to believe and teach.

QUESTION

How can prophets be deceived, as in the case of Mark Hoffman?

ANSWER

This question is simply another way of asking why prophets aren't infallible. It is doubtful that those asking the question suppose themselves obligated to be faultless. Why, then, do they suppose others must be? We do not believe in the infallibility of missionaries, or Sunday School teachers, or even bishops or stake presidents. At what point do we suppose infallibility must begin?

In a revelation dealing with the lost one hundred and sixteen pages of the Book of Mormon the Lord told Joseph Smith: "But as you cannot always judge the righteous, or as you cannot always tell the wicked from the righteous, therefore I say unto you, hold your peace until I shall see fit to make all things known unto the world concerning the matter" (D&C 10:37). If Joseph Smith had a weakness of character, it was in being too trusting and forgiving. Were we allowed to choose our own faults we would be hard pressed to do better than that.

We have the assurance that the man standing at the head of the Church will never lead it astray. We also have the promise that the united voice of the First Presidency and the Twelve will never err on matters that pertain to principles of salvation. The notion of infallibility, however, is not a part of our theology. In his preface to the Doctrine and Covenants the Lord said: "These commandments are of me, and were given unto my servants in their weakness, after the manner of their language, that they might come to understanding. And inasmuch as they erred it might be made known; and inasmuch as they sought wisdom they might be instructed; and inasmuch as they sinned they might be chastened, that they might repent; and inasmuch as they were humble they might be made strong, and blessed from on high, and receive knowledge from time to time" (D&C 1:24–28).

QUESTION

If we can't trust the judgment of the prophet in everything, how can we trust it in anything?

ANSWER

This chain of thought is used by fundamentalists who claim the Bible to be inerrant and infallible. Their argument is that if the Bible is in error on the smallest thing, be it a matter of science, history, geography, or whatever, we cannot possibly trust it when it speaks of Christ or gospel principles. All manner of contortions are necessary to maintain this position. It makes of their theology a pious fraud and constantly requires its adherent to lie, as it were, for God.

What if we assumed that a person who made a mistake on one matter could never to be trusted on another matter? Because we have all made mistakes, there would not be a soul left upon the face of the earth that we could trust. The irony of the argument of infallibility as it applies to the Bible is that those who make it cannot agree among themselves about what its various passages mean. Of what value is an infallible book among people whose interpretations of it are so terribly flawed?

The idea of infallibility simply doesn't work. Are children justified in rejecting the inspired counsel of their parents if they can show that on some other thing their parents erred? Can we set aside the counsel of a bishop if we know something of his own shortcomings? Can we disregard the instruction of the family physician if we discover he misdiagnosed an illness on some past occasion? Perfection is not requisite for trust, nor need we be perfect to enjoy the prompting of the Spirit or to share in the wisdom of heaven. Gratefully, that is the case, for were it not, none of us would be suitable for the Lord's service.

QUESTION

Isn't it racist or chauvinistic to believe that we are a chosen people?

ANSWER

In this day of egalitarianism when we are constantly reminded of the impropriety of supposing that a man can do anything better than a woman or that one race is superior to another, the idea that we as a church are a chosen people seems quite out of place and anything but politically correct. The idea of chosen people has its origin in the Old Testament. When the Lord formed the nation of Israel, he denominated them a chosen people (see Deuteronomy 7:6; 14:2; Exodus 19:5–6). In New Testament times Peter likewise designated those who united themselves with the Church of Jesus Christ (see 1 Peter 2:9). Thus we would assume that any religious body that professed to be the modern equivalent of the Lord's people would in like manner claim to be a chosen people.

In claiming to be a chosen people, we make no pretense to be superior to any other people but simply claim to have been chosen to serve as the Lord's messengers in declaring the message of salvation among the nations of the earth. Ours is a call to service, not to privilege, though the service itself is such. The promise given to Abraham was that his posterity would be called upon to bear the ministry and priesthood among all nations (see Abraham 2:9, 11). We claim to be the master of none and the servant of all. Elder

Neal A. Maxwell observed: "The designation 'chosen,' of course, is not just status; it confers great responsibilities upon those chosen to reach their fellowmen. God gives the picks and shovels to the 'chosen' because they are willing to go to work and get calluses on their hands. They may not be the best or most capable, but they are the most available" (*Deposition of a Disciple*, 54).

There is nothing elitist about this doctrine. The chosen of the Lord go to those of every nation, kindred, tongue, and people to declare the message of the restored gospel to all who will listen. Those who accept the message then join in and assume the responsibility to do their share in carrying the gospel message to others. In so doing they number themselves among the chosen of the Lord. All are welcome. None are denied, be they black or white, bond or free, male or female: "all are alike unto God" (2 Nephi 26:33).

QUESTION

Is it logical to suppose that we are literally Abraham's seed? Isn't this really figurative?

ANSWER

It seems logical or reasonable to suppose that we are literally the seed of Abraham if we accept the premise that there is a God in heaven who has a divine plan for his children. If, on the other hand, we assume that God has no interest in who marries whom and what children are born into a particular family, then there would be no logic to it. Perhaps the real question here is how important families are in the plan of salvation. When a man and woman go to the temple and are united as husband and wife for eternity and the Lord makes anew with them the covenant that he made with Abraham and Sarah relative to their posterity, would anyone suppose that he meant their "figurative" posterity rather than the literal seed of their union? What purpose would there be in making a promise to them that had nothing to do with them or their family?

The scriptures are both plain and emphatic in stating that the promise made to Abraham and Sarah was literal. "I give unto thee a promise," the Lord said, "that this right shall continue in thee, and in thy seed after thee (that is to say, the literal seed, or the seed of the body) shall all the families of the earth be blessed, even with the blessings of the Gospel, which are the blessings of salvation, even of life eternal" (Abraham 2:11). Speaking to Joseph Smith and the early elders of the Church the Lord said, "Ye are lawful heirs, according to the flesh, and have been hid from the world with Christ in God—therefore your life and the priesthood have remained, and must needs remain through you and your lineage until the restoration of all things spoken by the mouths of all the holy prophets since the world began" (D&C 86:9–10). To the Prophet the Lord said, "Abraham received promises concerning his seed, and of the fruit of his loins—from whose loins ye are, namely, my servant Joseph" (D&C 132:30). Language cannot be used more plainly to designate that these promises are literal, not figurative.

QUESTION

Do patriarchs declare lineage or assign it?

ANSWER

It is the office and calling of a patriarch in giving a patriarchal blessing to identify, by the Spirit of revelation, the blood lineage of those whom he blesses. President Joseph Fielding Smith taught: "A patriarch giving a blessing has the right of inspiration to declare the literal descent of the person receiving the blessing; he does not have authority to assign that individual to any tribe. Through the waters of baptism and the priesthood, Church members become heirs of Abraham with all the rights belonging to the children of Abraham through their faithfulness" (*Doctrines of Salvation*, 3:171).

The promises given to Abraham are not figurative. He was expressly told they were to extend to his "literal seed, or the seed of the body" (Abraham 2:11). If those of the Bible-believing world properly understood the promises given to Abraham, they would know that the blessings of the priesthood are essential to salvation and that the right to hold the priesthood was given to Abraham and his posterity. It is his seed that are to bear the message of the gospel to all the ends of the earth. Missionaries are expected to have received their patriarchal blessing before they begin their missions. Thus they will have a revealed confirmation that they are of the lineage that has a rightful claim to the priesthood and the attendant responsibility to declare the message of salvation to the ends of the earth.

QUESTION

What of those who are adopted into the house of Israel? Is there an actual change in their blood so that they and their posterity become literal descendants of Abraham?

ANSWER

Yes. The Prophet Joseph Smith said: "There are two Comforters spoken of. One is the Holy Ghost, the same as given on the day of Pentecost, and that all Saints receive after faith, repentance, and baptism. This first Comforter or Holy Ghost has no other effect than pure intelligence. It is more powerful in expanding the mind, enlightening the understanding, and storing the intellect with present knowledge, of a man who is of the literal seed of Abraham, than one that is a Gentile, though it may not have half as much visible effect upon the body; for as the Holy Ghost falls upon one of the literal seed of Abraham, it is calm and serene; and his whole soul and body are only exercised by the pure spirit of intelligence; while the effect of the Holy Ghost upon a Gentile, is to purge out the old blood, and make him actually of the seed of Abraham. That man that has none of the blood of Abraham (naturally) must have a new creation by the Holy Ghost. In such a case, there may be more of a powerful effect upon the body, and visible to the eye, than upon an Israelite, while the Israelite at first might be far before the Gentile in pure intelligence" (*Teachings of the Prophet Joseph Smith*, 149–50).

I have been repeatedly told that this statement is genetically and physiologically indefensible. That may well be the case, but then, so is the promise of a resurrection. I, for one, believe in both.

QUESTION

Why did God give Adam and Eve conflicting commandments in the Garden of Eden?

ANSWER

When God united Adam and Eve as husband and wife, he commanded them to "multiply, and replenish the earth" (Moses 2:28), something they could do only in a mortal state. He also commanded them not to partake of "the tree of the knowledge of good and evil" (Moses 3:17; see also 5:11; 2 Nephi 2:25). Nevertheless, he said, they would have their agency and could decide for themselves. Thus the stage was set for what we have come to know as the Fall. They could not keep either commandment without transgressing the other. Why would God have placed them in such a situation? Without detracting from the reality of the story, it also constitutes something of a type and shadow that foretells the kind of tests common to our earthly probation. Few faithful Latter-day Saints find themselves in the position of having to choose between good and evil. Those choices come, of course, but for Latter-day Saints no real choice exists in those circumstances. More common to the faithful is the choice between two seemingly good choices, both of which can be justified by gospel standards. For instance, consider the common choice made by parents about whether to accept an additional calling in the Church or excuse themselves from it because of family responsibilities. Both choices are good, but in each instance one represents the greater good.

Some years ago a young woman visited my office to seek counsel. She had come from India to study at Brigham Young University. While there she had been taught the gospel and was baptized. Not long thereafter her father called from India and told her to come home, that he and her mother had arranged a marriage for her according to the custom of their people. She told her father about joining the Church and her feelings of loyalty to it. He asked if the Church believed in the Ten Commandments. She assured him that it did. He then asked if the Church taught her to honor her father and mother. She replied that it did. He said, "Then I want you to honor me now by coming home and marrying according to the arrangement that your mother and I have made for you."

Her situation, not unlike many others, was not one of choosing between good and evil but of choosing between two things that were good—honoring her parents, and staying at school with the hope of finding someone to whom she could be married in the temple for time and eternity. Perhaps our greatest tests in mortality are found in those choices in which we demonstrate the wisdom and integrity to choose the greater good.

The conflicting commandments given to Adam and Eve created the opportunity for them to exercise their agency. With it came the opportunity to demonstrate their wisdom in choosing the greater over the lesser commandment.

QUESTION

Why did King Benjamin say that "the natural man is an enemy to God"? (Mosiah 3:19). We are children of our Father in Heaven, so shouldn't our natural tendencies be toward goodness?

ANSWER

King Benjamin's declaration that the natural man is an enemy to God does not address the question of whether the nature of mankind is inherently good or evil. The answer to that question depends on what man we are speaking of. The issue addressed by Benjamin is how the fall of Adam affects all who are born into this mortal or fallen world. This question must be answered correctly in order for us to properly understand the atonement of Christ. Said more simply, the Atonement comes in answer to the Fall, and if we do not fully understand our fallen state, we cannot fully understand the merit and value of our redemption in Christ.

Scripture teaches that at the time of our spirit birth, all of us were pure, innocent, and good. It could not be otherwise. The spirit is a creation of God in a literal, not a figurative, sense, and God does not create that which is evil. God granted to each of his spirit children the gift of agency that they might, through its proper use, become as he is. Through the misuse of that agency, some spirits became sufficiently evil and rebellious in our premortal estate that they with Lucifer, their leader, were cast out of the heavenly realms and denied the privilege of coming to earth to obtain a body and continue their progression toward godhood. These spirits we know as the devil and his angels. All others kept their first estate and merited the right to be born into this mortal life. Thus the scriptures tell us that "every spirit of man was innocent in the beginning; and God having redeemed man from the fall, men became again, in their infant state, innocent before God" (D&C 93:38). That is to say, as we were innocent at the time of our spirit birth, we became innocent once again at the time of our birth into mortality because of the atonement of Christ.

So the issue as far as the fallen nature of man is concerned is not whether we were born innocent, clean, or pure at birth. The scripture clearly states that we were. The issue is not whether our conception or birth was a sin. Again the scriptures are plain. God commanded Adam and Eve, and after them their posterity, in the proper union of marriage to multiply and replenish the earth. We could hardly argue that to keep a commandment is a sin. Thus the question becomes, Does acquiring a mortal, or fallen, body give Satan power over us, or does he gain power over us only when we choose to allow it through our own misdeeds? On this matter the scriptures are again plain.

The Lord told Adam that he had been forgiven for his "transgression in the Garden of Eden" (Moses 6:53). Thus the doctrine was established in that ancient day that "the sins of the parents cannot be answered upon the heads of the children, for they are whole from the foundation of the world" (Moses 6:54). Nevertheless, Adam was told that "children are conceived in sin, even so when they begin to grow up, sin conceiveth in their hearts, and they taste the bitter, that they may know to prize the good" (Moses 6:55).

How is a pure, perfect, and innocent child conceived in sin when no sin is associated with the act of conception? The answer is in the nature of the mortal, or fallen, body. Unlike the body possessed by their first parents while in Eden, all who are born into mortality have blood coursing in their veins. Blood brings death. To live in a mortal world is to know pain, aging, and death. None escape these lessons. Further, to be born into mortality is to be subject to "the god of this world" (2 Corinthians 4:4). It is to be subject to the effects of the flesh and to be under the dominion of him who rules over that which is of the flesh—that is, Satan. Thus conception becomes the means by which a mortal, or fallen, nature is transmitted to the posterity of Adam and Eve.

Lehi, in describing the mortal body, speaks of "the evil which is therein" (2 Nephi 2:29). Jacob invites all to reconcile themselves to God rather than submit "to the will of the devil and the flesh" (2 Nephi 10:24). Abinadi tells us that all mankind are "carnal, sensual, devilish" and that all would be lost were it not for the Atonement. "But remember," he said, "that he that persists in his own carnal nature, and goes on in the ways of sin and rebellion against God, remaineth in his fallen state [that state into which he was born] and the devil hath all power over him. Therefore he is as though there was no redemption made, being an enemy to God" (Mosiah 16:3–5).

Some would like to suppose that the tabernacle of flesh is neutral at the time of birth and remains so during that short period in which Satan is constrained from tempting little children. But this supposition does not accord with what the prophets of the Book of Mormon teach. It is clear that they understood, as did Adam, that we are conceived in sin, meaning into a body of flesh, which is subject to the adversary. Thus we must labor to be born again, or to live above the flesh, or we will be as though no redemption had been made.

King Benjamin tells us that little children, even though they are not subject to sin, are fallen by nature and can be saved only by Christ's atonement (see Mosiah 3:16). Mormon contrasted our mortal state with that of the three Nephites in their translated state. The change that came upon their bodies was such, he said, "that Satan could have no power over them, that he could not tempt them," for they had been "sanctified in the flesh, . . . that the powers of the earth could not hold them" (3 Nephi 28:39). Thus we see that the sinless child and the apostle of the Lord are both subjects of the kingdom of the flesh into which they were born, despite their loyalties to a greater King, and that they remain such until they are freed from this mortal probation.

To return to the idea that a correct understanding of the Fall is essential to a correct understanding of the Atonement, we see now that the child, even in its mother's womb, is subject to the effects of the Fall and is cut off from the presence of God. It in turn assures that the child is also a rightful heir of all blessings that are part of the atonement of Christ, for the Atonement answers the ends of the Fall. Thus, should a child die before birth or before it arrives at the age of accountability, it is assured salvation in the celestial kingdom (see D&C 137:10). It explains why mortals, even if they have been born again, cannot stand in the presence of God unless they are transfigured (see Moses 1:11; D&C 67:11–12). It explains why Moses, who had been in the presence of God and had repeatedly been addressed by him as "Moses, my son" and who had seen that he was in the "similitude of his Only Begotten," would say at the conclusion of such an experience, "for this cause I know that man is nothing, which thing I never had supposed. But now mine own eyes have beheld God; but not my natural, but my spiritual eyes, for my natural eyes could not have beheld; for I should have withered and died in his presence; but his glory was upon me; and I beheld his face, for I was transfigured before him" (Moses 1:6, 7, 10–11, 13). Thus, like Moses, we learn that without the atonement of Christ and without the glory that only God can place on the physical body, we too are nothing.

QUESTION

In Alma 32 we learn that when we have knowledge, our faith becomes dormant. If God has all knowledge, as the scriptures tell us, can he have faith?

ANSWER

In the *Lectures on Faith*, Joseph Smith taught us that if it were not for the principle of faith, as that principle is found in God, the worlds would not have been framed nor man created. Faith, we are told, "is the principle by which Jehovah works, and through which he exercises power over all temporal as well as eternal things. Take this principle or attribute—for it is an attribute—from the Deity, and he would cease to exist" (*Lecture* 1:16). Without question God has faith and does all that he does by that power. How then do we reconcile this knowledge with Alma's reasoning that when your knowledge of a particular thing becomes perfect, your faith on that matter becomes dormant? (see Alma 32:34).

All teaching, if it is to be understood, must be done at the level of those being taught. Thus we may answer a question differently for students on an elementary level than we would if the students were on a college or graduate level. Similarly, our purpose and perspective in answering a question dictates what we teach. For instance, if we are defining priesthood from man's perspective, we would say that it is the power and authority of God delegated to man to act in God's name. If we were defining priesthood from God's perspective, we would not speak of delegated authority, for God does not act in someone else's name. We would simply define priesthood as God's power and authority.

Just as man and God define priesthood differently, so do they define faith differently. Little that we say of faith as it functions in our lives is true of how it functions in God's life. For instance, we can increase in faith; God cannot. We can lose faith; God cannot. We can substitute faith for knowledge; God cannot. Thus, in defining faith we generally speak from our perspective, as Alma does in teaching the Zoramites. He is teaching a group of people whose understanding of the principle of faith is that of an elementary school class; Joseph Smith is teaching the School of the Prophets. Alma's purpose is to encourage those he is teaching to begin the process by which they can advance from grace to grace, or from one level of faith to a greater level of faith. Joseph Smith, on the other hand, is addressing men of faith and understanding. He is attempting to give them a more expansive view of the operation of faith as it is manifest in all that God does. He speaks of faith as it is known to the Gods, as the "great governing principle which has power, dominion, and authority over all things" (*Lecture* 1:24). Alma and Joseph Smith are not in disagreement with each other; they are simply emphasizing different aspects of faith suited to the level of those they are teaching.

QUESTION

What do you do when you receive no answer to your prayers?

ANSWER

Keep praying. In the meantime, listen more closely so that if an answer is being given, you are not missing it. This procedure can be particularly important when you are strongly disposed to justify a particular course of action. Be willing to hear what you may not want to hear. A searching interview of yourself may also be in order to assure that you have not offended the Spirit, thus causing it to withdraw. Having done these things and a deadline requires that you choose a course of action, counsel with the Lord and proceed. If you have made the wrong choice, trust the Lord to intervene before your course becomes irreversible.

If you ask God for direction on a matter and don't receive it, of necessity you must proceed and do the best you can. Brigham Young assured us that in such circumstances, God is bound to honor what we have done and testified that he will do so (see *Journal of Discourses*, 3:205).

AT ISSUE

Everyone has unanswered questions. Were it not so, the purposes of mortality would not be served. We came into this life to be tested and to learn to walk by faith. Such a test would not be possible if all our questions were answered. For this same reason, we have no obligation to answer every question that can be asked about our faith, nor do we have the obligation to respond to every objection that can be raised. Those seeking reason to reject Christ and his gospel have always found it. Those seeking reason for faith have always been richly rewarded.

CHAPTER ELEVEN

UNDERSTANDING SCRIPTURE

What is the secret to effective scripture study?

By what rule of thumb do we distinguish between that which is literal and that which is figurative in scripture?

The eighth Article of Faith states: "We believe the Bible to be the word of God as far as it is translated correctly." Are there mistranslations of the Bible that we ought be warned about?

What is the significance of the Joseph Smith Translation, and did Joseph Smith complete his work on it?

Why do we use the King James Version of the Bible when its language is so archaic and modern scholarship has given us improved translations?

Is it possible to truly believe the Bible without believing the Book of Mormon and the other revelations of the Restoration if you become acquainted with them?

Isn't it unfair for Latter-day Saints to read Mormonism into the Old and New Testaments?

What role, if any, should scripture commentaries play in our study?

Is everything that is said in general conference scripture?

SCRIPTURE WHICH IS THE MIND, the will, and the word of the Lord can only be understood to the extent that our thought process is one with his. It has been properly said that it takes scripture to understand scripture, meaning it takes the Spirit to understand the things of the Spirit. Our faith must not be based, as the apostle Paul observed, in the wisdom of the world. "We speak the wisdom of God in a mystery," he said, "even the hidden wisdom, which God ordained before the world unto our glory" (1 Corinthians 2:7). Such things can only be known by the Spirit of revelation. "For what man knoweth the things of a man, save the spirit of man which is in him? even so the things of God knoweth no man, but the Spirit of God. Now we have received, not the spirit of the world, but the spirit which is of God; that we might know the things that are freely given to us of God. Which things also we speak, not in the words which man's wisdom teacheth, but which the Holy Ghost teacheth; comparing spiritual things with spiritual. But the natural man receiveth not the things of the Spirit of God: for they are foolishness unto him: neither can he know them, because they are spiritually discerned" (1 Corinthians 2:11–14).

Addressing the issue of how we are to obtain an understanding of the gospel, the Lord asks of those who have been called to teach and preach: "Unto what were ye ordained?" In response to his own question he declares: "To preach my gospel by the Spirit, even the Comforter which was sent forth to teach the truth" (D&C 50:13–14). Thus to be true to the calling to declare the gospel, we must be true to the gospel and true to the Spirit. That is, we must teach the gospel of Jesus Christ and none other, and it must be taught by his Spirit and none other. If the gospel should be taught in some other way, the Lord declared, "It is not of God" (D&C 50:18). Then addressing himself to those who desire to learn the truths of the gospel, he asks: "And again, he that receiveth the word of truth, doth he receive it by the Spirit of truth or some other way?" Then in harmony with the answer and the spirit of the previous question, he says, "If it be some other way it is not of God" (D&C 50:19–20).

"If ye receive not the Spirit ye shall not teach," the revelation known as the law of the Lord declares (D&C 42:14). In like manner, we might add, If ye have not the Spirit ye shall not learn. "Therefore, why is it that ye cannot understand and know, that he that receiveth the word by the Spirit of truth receiveth it as it is preached by the Spirit of truth? Wherefore, he that preacheth and he that receiveth, understand one another, and both are edified and rejoice together" (D&C 50:21–22).

Inseparably connected with the verity that the things of the Spirit can only be understood by the Spirit is another eternal truth, namely, that the "powers of heaven [which include an understanding of all gospel principles] cannot be controlled nor handled only upon the principles of righteousness" (D&C 121:36). The temple, for instance, is a house of learning but only to those who enter it worthily. Only if a man does the will of the Father can he know the doctrine of the Father (see John 7:17). As obedience brings light and truth, so it is lost in transgression (see D&C 93:39). "I will give unto the children of men line upon line, precept upon precept, here a little and there a little; and blessed are those who hearken unto my precepts, and lend an ear unto my counsel, for they shall learn wisdom; for unto him that receiveth I will give more; and from them that shall say, We have enough, from them shall be taken away even that which they have" (2 Nephi 28:30). Only in righteousness can one obtain the "key of the knowledge of God" (D&C 84:19), and only by loyalty to the revelations of the Restoration can that key be turned. The tombs of Egypt may yield the writings of ancient prophets, but it is only by the "gift and power of God" that they may be translated (Omni 1:20).

Our revelations speak of a condemnation that rests upon the whole Church because we have treated lightly the revelations that have been given us (see D&C 84:54–61). Yet to those who faithfully sustain the prophet the Lord has said, "God shall give unto you knowledge by his Holy Spirit, yea, by the unspeakable gift of the Holy Ghost, that has not been revealed since the world was until now" (D&C 121:26).

To all of this we add the reminder from Peter that "no prophecy of the scripture is of any private interpretation" (2 Peter 1:20), meaning that scripture is not open to a variety of conflicting views. Scripture can mean only what God intended it to mean.

With the help of such instruction we can form the following rules of scriptural interpretation:

1. An understanding of the basic principles of the gospel is essential to understanding the scriptures.

2. Spiritual truths can only be understood by the aid of the Spirit.

3. A knowledge of the things of the Spirit was planted in our hearts long before we were born. Thus there is a spirit of familiarity in all saving truths. When we hear them, it is as if we always knew them.

4. Spiritual truths will always be in harmony with themselves and each other and often, if not always, at odds with the doctrines of men.

5. Proper understanding of scripture requires obedience to gospel standards. Living gospel principles is essential to understanding gospel principles.

6. Our understanding of gospel truths cannot remain static. It either becomes "brighter and brighter until the perfect day" (D&C 50:24) or it becomes dimmer and dimmer until all is lost.

7. The revelations of the Restoration are the key to unlocking the true meaning of the Old and New Testaments.

8. No prophecy or scripture means anything other than what God intended it to mean. It cannot properly be used to sustain conflicting views. One cannot, for instance, properly understand the true meaning of the Bible and at the same time maintain membership in any church other than the church that the Lord

has designated as the "only true and living church upon the face of the whole earth" (D&C 1:30).

QUESTION

What is the secret to effective scripture study?

ANSWER

The great and grand secret is that there is no secret. Effective scripture study is not found in color-coding various passages, in systems of underlining, or in methods of cross-referencing. It is not a matter of whether things are studied chronologically or topically, daily or every other day. It is not found in possessing a knowledge of Hebrew or Greek, nor does one obtain it through the latest compilation of books on a computer disk. The answer is found where many would rather that it not be. It is found in uniting consistency and intensity with the quiet prompting of the Spirit—a Spirit known only to those who are both consistent and intense in their study. It is the blessing granted to those who quietly dig, and chisel and hammer away in countless hours of scripture study. It is the privilege of those who learn things well enough to teach them and who, in teaching, trust the Spirit and the power of holy writ to give life and meaning to that which they teach. It is the privilege of those who ponder and search, who savor and trust and plod. Such come to know the Spirit of scripture.

"I hope each of you has had the same experience that has been mine on many occasions," observed Elder Bruce R. McConkie. "In the spirit of prayer, while reading and pondering the holy word, new views, added concepts, truths theretofore unknown, have suddenly dawned upon me. Doctrines that were dim and hidden and little known have, in an instant, been shown forth with greater clarity and in wondrous beauty. This is exactly what happened to President Joseph F. Smith when he received the vision of the redemption of the dead. I hope each of you has had the experience, while preaching upon scriptural passages, of having a sudden rush of ideas which gave you a far greater comprehension of the doctrine you were then teaching. We are all entitled to this spirit of prophecy and of revelation" (leadership training meeting, 2 October 1981).

QUESTION

By what rule of thumb do we distinguish between that which is literal and that which is figurative in scripture?

ANSWER

This matter is of utmost importance in scriptural interpretation. Consider that the declaration that humankind were created in the image and likeness of God is held to be a metaphor by all but Latter-day Saints. Our testimony that Jesus Christ is the literal Son of God is one of the reasons the traditional Christian world declares Mormonism to be a non-Christian cult. The idea that God is actually a personal being—one with body, parts, and passions—and that he is actually the father of our spirits makes Latter-day Saints heretics, according to historical Christianity. Again, one part of the Christian world rejects the necessity of baptism, claiming it to be merely an outward manifestation of an inward conviction, and another holds there is no salvation without it. To some in the Christian world partaking of the sacrament is literally to eat the flesh and drink the blood of Christ. Many in both the Catholic and the Protestant worlds claim Adam and Eve to be mythic creatures devised by a primitive people to explain their otherwise mysterious origins. And of course the many appearances of God to his prophets, as recorded in scripture, are held by Catholic, Protestant, and Jew alike to be metaphorical because "no man hath seen God at any time" (John 1:18).

The traditional Christian world has so completely turned upside down the meaning of everything in holy writ that the

Oxford Dictionary of the Christian Church under the heading "God" states that "all affirmations of Scripture and the Fathers [Christian scholars of the second century] are but metaphors devised for the ignorant" (Cross, ed., 576).

Virtually every tenet of our faith represents a departure from the theological position of historical or traditional Christianity. What we declare to be literal, they declare to be figurative; what we declare to be figurative, they declare to be literal. Thus we share a common vocabulary while holding to an entirely different set of meanings. This same division of understanding is also common between ministers of the various faiths and their parishioners, the one having been schooled in philosophical speculations and the other following the scripture of the heart and the plain meaning of words. Most of the people our missionaries teach share a faith in common with us but suppose it to originate with their church. They are very surprised to find out that it doesn't. In fact, their faith represents feelings and understanding they brought with them from their first estate. A recent convert observed at her baptism that she always knew the Church was true; she only needed the missionaries to show her where it was.

Of necessity, doctrines of salvation must be a matter of revelation, not of speculation. The book of Genesis declares Adam to have been created from the "dust of the ground" (Genesis 2:7). Modern revelation tells us that all mankind were also created from the dust of the earth (see Mormon 9:17; Moses 6:59). Those in the household of faith are entitled to see beyond the metaphor and know that Adam "was the son of God" (Moses 6:22), or as Abraham states it, the "firstborn" of God's children into mortality (Abraham 1:3). Joseph Smith asked: "Was there ever a son without a father?" to which he responded, "Whenever did a tree or anything spring into existence without a progenitor? And everything comes in this way" (*Teachings of the Prophet Joseph Smith*, 373). The psalmist said that the "meek shall inherit the earth" (Psalm 37:11). Christ repeated the promise in the Sermon on the

Mount (see Matthew 5:5). Modern revelation declares it to be literally so, adding that "the righteous shall inherit it" in its sanctified and glorified state (D&C 88:26; see also v. 17). In the Sermon on the Mount we are also told that the pure in heart shall see God (see Matthew 5:8). Modern revelation affirms the promise to be literal. "Verily, thus saith the Lord," begins a revelation given to the Prophet Joseph Smith in May 1833, "it shall come to pass that every soul who forsaketh his sins and cometh unto me, and calleth on my name, and obeyeth my voice, and keepeth my commandments, shall see my face and know that I am" (D&C 93:1).

Many other examples could be cited to illustrate the importance of modern revelation in affirming the literal nature of Bible statements. There are, however, many instances in which no revealed help is given. In such cases we must rely on our own common sense and the measure of inspiration that is ours. As an illustration, consider the following text: "Hear, O Israel: The Lord our God is one Lord: And thou shalt love the Lord thy God with all thine heart, and with all thy soul, and with all thy might. And these words, which I command thee this day, shall be in thine heart: and thou shalt teach them diligently unto thy children, and shalt talk of them when thou sittest in thine house, and when thou walkest by the way, and when thou liest down, and when thou risest up. And thou shalt bind them for a sign upon thine hand, and they shall be as frontlets between thine eyes. And thou shalt write them upon the posts of thy house, and on thy gates" (Deuteronomy 6:4–9).

Out of this text comes the Jewish tradition of wearing phylacteries—two small leather boxes, each containing strips of parchment inscribed with the above quotation, one of which is strapped to the forehead and the other to the left arm during morning prayer—and the mezuzot, a small container nailed to the right-hand doorpost or gate, which also contains a copy of this text. While agreeing with the importance of the text, we as Latter-day Saints have not supposed that God intended such a literal interpretation of it. We do believe that God literally appeared to Moses on Mount Sinai, whereas the idea of an anthropomorphic God is offensive to the tradition of Jew and Christian alike.

The interpretation we put on any scriptural text is a measure of our spiritual integrity. In principle it is no different from the way we choose to act when we hear the message of the gospel preached. The revelations declare that the earth has seven thousand years of temporal history, yet there are those anxious to harmonize the scriptures with the theories of science who maintain that the years in these texts are symbolic and couldn't possibly mean what they say. Likewise, there are those who are offended by the idea that we as Latter-day Saints literally have the blood of Abraham. Scientifically and statistically, we are told, there is no way that this is possible. (Again we observe that science and statistics also deny the possibility of a corporeal resurrection.) Thus they hold that even though the scripture declares we are the literal seed of Abraham, the scripture could not possibly mean what it says (see Abraham 2:11). Interpretations of this sort stand or fall on their own merit, and though volumes could be written on the subject, no sure system or guide can be given for discerning the figurative from the literal. On this matter, as with so many others, eventually we must rely on our own good sense and the measure of the Spirit that is ours.

QUESTION

The eighth Article of Faith states: "We believe the Bible to be the word of God as far as it is translated correctly." Are there mistranslations of the Bible that we ought be warned about?

ANSWER

All serious students of the Bible, regardless of church affiliation, ought to share an equal concern that the Bible be translated correctly and freely join hands in any labor that leads to that end.

Latter-day Saints have frequently been criticized for Joseph Smith's suggestion that there were difficulties in the translation of the Bible extant in his day. Yet, significantly, the Bible-believing world—Catholics and Protestants alike—have witnessed a near-deluge of Bible translations since the days of Joseph Smith. A work entitled *So Many Versions?* published in 1975, lists 158 English translations of the Bible made in this century alone. The past twenty years have certainly witnessed no slowing in that process.

Joseph Smith, however, was primarily concerned with things that had been taken from the Bible, not problems of translation. While he was translating the Book of Mormon, the Prophet became acquainted with Nephi's prophetic description of what would happen to the Bible. Nephi affirmed that as originally written it contained "the fulness of the gospel of the Lord," but that when it passed through the hands of the "great and abominable church," evil and designing men took from it "many parts which [were] plain and most precious; and also many covenants of the Lord" (1 Nephi 13:24, 26). Only after these plain and precious parts had been taken did the book go forth to the nations of the earth. Because of that which had been taken, Nephi explained, "an exceedingly great many do stumble, yea, insomuch that Satan hath great power over them" (1 Nephi 13:29).

From the revelations he received in restoring the gospel, the Prophet observed: "It was apparent that many important points touching the salvation of man had been taken from the Bible, or lost before it was compiled" (headnote to D&C 76). A comparison of the first few chapters of Genesis with the book of Moses illustrates the point. In textual restorations made by the Prophet, we learn that Adam had the fulness of the gospel of Jesus Christ, that he was baptized, received the gift of the Holy Ghost, held the priesthood, and did all things in the name of the Son of God. In these same chapters we learn of the panoramic vision shown to Enoch, including the restoration of the gospel in the last days, the coming forth of the Book of Mormon, the building of the New

Jerusalem, and Enoch's city coming down out of heaven during the millennial day (see Moses 7:62–64). We also learn that the doctrine taught by Noah before the Flood was of faith in Jesus Christ, the Son of God, repentance, baptism, and the receipt of the Holy Ghost with the attendant promise of revelation (see Moses 8:24).

Both the doctrines and their plainness as found in the Book of Mormon and the Doctrine and Covenants illustrate how the Bible should read. These are not translation difficulties being corrected. They represent the restoration of plain and precious truths deliberately taken from the sacred text that falsehoods might be perpetuated and that men might stumble. They come to us as a part of the restoration of all things.

QUESTION

What is the significance of the Joseph Smith Translation, and did Joseph Smith complete his work on it?

ANSWER

The Joseph Smith Translation of the Bible is a significant witness of the divine mission of the Prophet Joseph Smith. The Prophet spoke and wrote as one having authority. At his hand more truths and knowledge about Christ are available to the honest seeker of truth than by the labors of any other man who ever lived. Among the particular contributions of the Joseph Smith Translation are the many marvelous texts that restore to us the knowledge that the prophets of the Old Testament, beginning with father Adam, testified of Christ and enjoyed a knowledge of the fulness of his gospel. Joseph Smith's labor gives more clarity, power, and purpose to the Old Testament than do those of all the scholars in earth's history combined.

The Joseph Smith Translation is the most complete and perfect Bible translation ever known to the world. It contains thousands of additions to and clarifications of the King James

Version. Many of the revelations in the Doctrine and Covenants came as the Prophet labored over difficulties presented by Old and New Testament texts. The book of Moses and Joseph Smith–Matthew in the Pearl of Great Price are both extracts from the Joseph Smith Translation and are priceless contributions to our understanding of Genesis and Matthew. Much that was taken from the Bible by evil and designing men has been restored to us in the Joseph Smith Translation. It, combined with the revelations that grew out of its translation and are now recorded in the Doctrine and Covenants, gives us a wealth of information lost to the world. Nor does the story stop here, for through these revelations we also obtain much understanding that was not had even in ancient days.

As to whether the Joseph Smith Translation is complete, it ought to be observed that no compilation of scriptural texts can ever circumscribe the Spirit of revelation. There is nothing in all of holy writ to which more of the light of heaven could not be added. "That which is of God is light; and he that receiveth light, and continueth in God, receiveth more light; and that light groweth brighter and brighter until the perfect day" (D&C 50:24). Joseph Smith did get through the entire Bible from Genesis to Revelation by July 1833; however, he did not make all the changes that were needed or that he desired to make. The Prophet contin-ued work on his translation of the Bible up to the time of his death.

QUESTION

Why do we use the King James Version of the Bible when its language is so archaic and modern scholarship has given us improved translations?

ANSWER

The King James Version is the Bible of the Restoration. It is the Bible that Joseph Smith used as a style guide for translating the

Book of Mormon and the revelations he received as they are recorded in the Doctrine and Covenants. The gospel as restored to Joseph Smith represents the fulfillment of a great host of promises made by the prophets of the Old and New Testaments. The revelations of the Restoration pick up the language of these prophecies as found in the King James Bible to announce their fulfillment or to amplify or extend them. Thus the Bible or the testimony of the ancients becomes one with the revelations given in our day. They weave themselves together as part of the same tapestry and become, as it was prophesied they would, one in our hands (see Ezekiel 37:19; 2 Nephi 3:12).

For example, the New English Bible tells us that Elijah would come to "reconcile fathers to sons and sons to fathers, lest I [the Lord] come and put the land under a ban to destroy it" (NEB Malachi 4:6). A reconciliation between fathers and sons to prevent the destruction of their land neither conveys Malachi's intended message nor justifies the return of Elijah. If this was the language we were familiar with, we would miss the tie between it and the rendering of this verse by Moroni when he quoted Malachi as saying, "Behold, I will reveal unto you the Priesthood, by the hand of Elijah the prophet. . . . And he shall plant in the hearts of the children the promises made to the fathers, and the hearts of the children shall turn to their fathers. If it were not so, the whole earth would be utterly wasted at his coming" (Joseph Smith–History 1:38–39).

In the revelation on the degrees of glory, those who obtain their exaltation are spoken of as "priests and kings" (D&C 76:56). The King James Bible contains a companion passage in Revelation 5:10, whereas the New English Bible simply speaks of them as priests with no suggestion that they are kings and would thus have claim on a kingdom of some sort or another. Similarly, the phrase a "more sure word of prophecy" used by Peter (2 Peter 1:19) and explained by the Prophet in Doctrine and Covenants 131:5 is not found in the New English Bible. Theologically, a great deal is being lost in these and many like instances.

QUESTION

Is it possible to truly believe the Bible without believing the Book of Mormon and the other revelations of the Restoration if you become acquainted with them?

ANSWER

Is it possible to believe the Old Testament and at the same time reject the testimony that Jesus of Nazareth is the Christ? Is it possible to accept the reality of the characters of the Old Testament and the veracity of its stories, embrace its principles and practices, profess a great love for it, memorize passages from it, preach from it, and yet miss the heart of its message, which is to testify of Christ? Many in the world today profess faith in the Old Testament while rejecting the testimony of Christ. How strange that so many reverence the book while rejecting its Author. In like manner, we ask, Is it possible to accept the New Testament or the teachings of Christ in the Old World while rejecting his teachings as they have come to us from the New World? Could one possibly be true and the other false?

Mormon, the prophet after whom the Book of Mormon is named, bore this testimony: "For behold, this [the Book of Mormon] is written for the intent that ye may believe that [the Bible]; and if ye believe that ye will believe this also; and if ye believe this ye will know concerning your fathers, and also the marvelous works which were wrought by the power of God among them" (Mormon 7:9). Similarly, Nephi, the son of Lehi, reasoned thus: "And now, my beloved brethren, and also Jew, and all ye ends of the earth, hearken unto these words and believe in Christ; and if ye believe not in these words believe in Christ. And if ye shall believe in Christ ye will believe in these words, for they are the words of Christ, and he hath given them unto me; and they teach all men that they should do good" (2 Nephi 33:10).

At issue here is the message, not the messenger. If both the Bible and the Book of Mormon come from the same source, then to reject either is to reject the source. The Judgment will not center in the dispensation in which we lived but in our acceptance of the divine message, which is the same in all dispensations. If the Lord sends that message to us in the mouth of two witnesses, we are expected to accept them both; if he sends three witnesses, we are expected to accept all three. What we cannot do is choose among the witnesses any more than we can choose among the passages of scripture which we will believe or among the ordinances of salvation which we will comply with.

QUESTION

Isn't it unfair for Latter-day Saints to read Mormonism into the Old and New Testaments?

ANSWER

No one in the Christian world would suppose it unfair to read their knowledge and testimony of Christ into the prophecies of the Old Testament. For them to fail to do so would be to deny their testimony of Christ and the explanations he gave of the scriptures. Likewise, for Latter-day Saints to fail to read their testimony of the restored gospel into the Old and New Testament would represent a denial of that which Christ has revealed and restored to us. Take, for example, the appearance of John the Baptist to Joseph Smith and Oliver Cowdery. Explaining that he acted under the direction of Peter, James, and John, who held the keys of the Melchizedek Priesthood, John the Baptist laid his hands upon the heads of Joseph Smith and Oliver Cowdery and conferred upon them both the Aaronic Priesthood and its keys. He committed to them the authority to preach the gospel of repentance and to perform baptisms by immersion for the remission of sins. He granted them the right to receive the ministration of angels and the authority by which the sons of Levi would yet offer an offering in righteousness to the Lord. He also instructed Joseph and Oliver to baptize each other in the Susquehanna River and then directed them to reordain each other to the priesthood. We assume that he oversaw these events to ensure that they were done properly (see Joseph Smith–History 1:68–75).

Now, having embraced all this as part of our faith, are we not bound by the tenets of that faith to believe that baptism was an essential ordinance of the gospel of Christ in New Testament times? Are we not obligated to believe that a legal and lawful baptism required an administrator who held the priesthood? Would we not be obligated to believe that the baptisms were performed by immersion? Could we suppose that the meridian Saints did not experience the administration of angels or that they did not believe the office of the Levitical Priesthood and the ordinances performed by the sons of Levi would yet have a proper place in their faith? Could we suppose that salvation was to be by grace alone—that the doctrine of repentance was not essential or that ordinances were not necessary? Upon which of these principles can we in good faith act as if we had not been given light and understanding? Upon which of these matters could we join the confusion common to the traditional Christian world, acting as if we did not know what was truly happening in the New Testament?

We could only suppose that for us to fail to see the story of the New Testament in the light of the restored gospel and acting as if we did not have the knowledge granted us would be both offensive to the Spirit and destructive to the testimony we profess.

QUESTION

What role, if any, should scripture commentaries play in our study?

ANSWER

If we did not need encouragement in living the gospel and help in understanding and applying the scriptures, we would not have speakers in sacrament meetings nor would we have Sunday School, priesthood, Relief Society, or Primary classes. We certainly wouldn't need a three-hour block of meetings on Sunday. Nor would we have seminary and institute classes, firesides, or any of the host of other activities designed to increase our gospel understanding. If the written word was not as important as the spoken word, we would not have Church magazines, manuals, or the *Church News*. The purpose for each of these meetings and publications is to comment on gospel principles and encourage gospel living.

In fact, much of scripture, and this is particularly true of the teachings of the Savior, is commentary on other scripture. The issue is not really if we need help in understanding the scriptures but rather what the most reliable sources of help are. The answer is anything that can trace itself to the Holy Ghost. All sources must stand on their own merit. If their authorship evidences a testimony of the Restoration, an understanding of the scriptures, a spirit that sustains doctrines of the Church and the direction given it by its leaders, the materials may well add to our understanding. It would be a little strange to say that people can answer questions or teach the gospel orally but not in writing. The Spirit of the Lord can confirm or warn against that which is written as easily as it does with that which is spoken.

The Bible, the Book of Mormon, the Doctrine and Covenants, and the Pearl of Great Price are known as the standard works—so called because they constitute the standard by which we judge all other sources. Yet ours is a true and living Church, which means that the Spirit of revelation must always be found among us. It is by the light of that Spirit that we seek both new scripture and an expanded understanding of the scripture we have.

QUESTION

Is everything that is said in general conference scripture?

ANSWER

Anything spoken under the direction of the Holy Ghost is scripture. Scripture is scripture because it represents the mind, the will, and the word of the Lord, not because it was uttered in a particular place (see D&C 68:4). The standard works contain a selection of revelations or scriptural utterances that are the standard in directing and governing the Church.

Our general conferences are a source of renewed spiritual strength. In both music and the spoken word they set a pattern for instructional meetings. Though perhaps not all that is spoken in general conference can claim to represent the voice of the Lord, surely much of it can.

AT ISSUE

Every time we interpret or apply a scripture, the Lord gets a measure of our spiritual maturity and integrity. As scripture has prompted immeasurable good, so has it been used to justify all manner of wickedness. Just as no other book in earth's history has been misquoted or misused more frequently than the Holy Bible, so no other book has been the source of more righteousness and goodness. Mortality is a test, and the interpretation of scripture is an important part of that test.

No issue in scriptural interpretation is more important than distinguishing between what is figurative and what is literal. No sure rule or standard can be given in making such judgments. As with everything in holy writ, the Spirit must be our guide and our conclusions the measure of sense and loyalty to the gospel cause.

No single thing will do more to unlock our understanding of the Old and New Testaments than becoming competent students of the revelations of the Restoration. Because the gospel is the same yesterday, today, and forever, its principles being eternal, virtually every revelation given in our dispensation is an inspired commentary on the revelations of the past. To fail to study the past through the Urim and Thummim of the present—that is, through the revelations that restore the gospel known to the ancients—is to deny the Spirit by which all revealed truth comes.

CHAPTER TWELVE

IS THAT DOCTRINE?

How do we distinguish the doctrine of the Church from that which is not
  doctrine?

Does the gospel embrace all truth?

Does doctrine change?

Who can declare doctrine?

When we teach, is it ever proper to go beyond the literal rendering of the
  scripture itself?

Are all the answers we need found in the scriptures?

How should doctrinal issues be settled?

I T IS NOT UNCOMMON IN gospel discussions for someone to chal-
lenge what is being said with the question, "Is that official
Church doctrine?" This question often means the one asking it
does not like what is being said and is seeking a reason not to be
bound by it. The question is generally successful in putting the one
being challenged on the defensive because of the difficulties associated with defining "official Church doctrine." In telling the story
of the Creation, for instance, teachers are commonly challenged

with the question, "Does the Church have an official position on the theory of evolution?" The answer is no, it does not. On the other hand, and this is certainly very important in such a discussion, the Church does have an official position on the doctrine of the origin of man. The way questions are framed is very important. On the one hand, the Church is not in the business of evaluating scientific theories; on the other, it is in the business of teaching that all humankind are the offspring of divine parents and thus not the product of an evolutionary process. The knowledge that we obtain in the temple, knowledge required for us to enter into the presence of the Lord, and the ordinances performed there do not permit the notion that our blood line traces to animals.

If the body of "official doctrine" is to be limited to formal declarations by the First Presidency, the Church has precious little doctrine. From the time of its organization in the spring of 1830 to the present, there have been very few instances in which the First Presidency has issued "official" doctrinal declarations. These have included the statement on the origin of man, a doctrinal exposition on the Father and the Son, and most recently the proclamation on the family. Each of these declarations is marvelous in its own right, but if our definition of "official doctrines" is defined so narrowly that it is limited to these declarations and the few others we have received, we could not even declare faith, repentance, and baptism as doctrines of the Church. Indeed, most of what we understand to be the doctrine of the Church finds no mention in such documents. Certainly the standard works, the temple ceremony, and much instruction that has come to us by those whom we sustain as prophets, seers, and revelators is also "official doctrine."

The difficulties in defining doctrine too narrowly are matched by those that are too broad and sweeping. For instance, it is not uncommon to hear someone say that anything taught in general conference is "official doctrine." Such a standard makes the place where something is said rather than what is said the standard of truth. Nor is something doctrine simply because it was said by someone who holds a particular office or position. Truth is not an office or a position to which one is ordained. Let us examine some points that will help clarify what things are or are not doctrine.

QUESTION

How do we distinguish the doctrine of the Church from that which is not doctrine?

ANSWER

Perhaps the safest way to answer this question is to identify the characteristics that are common to good doctrine. They include the following:

First, good doctrine will always sustain the idea that the living prophet, not scripture or any other document, is the constitution of the Church. The Church is not governed by canon law, we have no creed to which we must pay allegiance, nor do we have a written constitution. The governing authority of the Church is the voice of the living prophet. It must ever be so. Our faith embraces "all that God has revealed, all that He does now reveal, and we believe that He will yet reveal many great and important things pertaining to the Kingdom of God" (Article of Faith 9). The man who stands at the head of the Church is the instrument through which the Lord conveys the doctrine that is to bind the Church as a whole. Perhaps the following illustration will help.

Some time ago I received a long-distance call from a missionary serving in Texas. He had been given material produced by anti-Mormons declaring that Latter-day Saints believe that Adam is God. "What's the deal?" he asked with considerable excitement in his voice.

"Elder," I asked, "were you born and raised in the Church?"

"Yes," he said.

"Did you attend seminary?"

"Yes."

"Have you ever had an institute class?"

"A few," he said.

"Do you read the Church magazines?"

"Yes."

"Have you read the standard works?"

"Yes."

"Do you listen to general conference?"

"Yes." The tone of his voice now contained a hint of exasperation.

"Well, then," I said, "in all that you have read and been taught, how many times have you been told that Latter-day Saints believe that Adam is God?"

"Never," he said a little sharply.

"What do you suppose the reason for that is?" I asked.

"I don't know," the missionary said.

"Well, then," I said, "could the reason you were never taught such a thing in Sunday School, or sacrament meeting, or priesthood meetings, or seminary, or your institute classes, or stake conference, or general conferences, or in Church magazines, or in the scriptures be because we as Latter-day Saints don't believe it?"

"Well," he said, "it says here that Brigham Young taught it."

"Elder," I asked, "is the issue whether Brigham Young taught it or whether it is a doctrine of the Church?"

"Both," he said.

"All right, let's take first the issue of whether it's the doctrine of the Church. We have about ten million members of the Church. Do you suppose that a single one of them has been taught in any Church class or meeting that Adam was God?"

"No."

"Why not?"

"Because we don't believe that," the missionary replied.

"There is an important point in all of this, Elder," I said. "Never let anyone outside the Church tell you what the Church teaches. You were sent out to teach, not to be taught (see D&C 43:15). The doctrines of the Church will always come to you through the channels that the Lord ordained, and the Lord didn't ordain anti-Mormon literature as one of those channels."

"Okay," he said, "but did Brigham Young teach such a thing?"

"I don't know what the pamphlet you have attributes to Brigham Young," I said, "but I don't think that is the real issue. Brigham Young taught a host of eternal truths in which this pamphleteer has no interest. That has to tell us something about the pamphleteer. His is not a search for truth; it is a search for something to quibble about. He is building what we call a straw man."

"What is a straw man?" he asked.

"To build a straw man, your critic takes something he knows he can pound the stuffing out of, and he attributes it to you as your belief. He then beats it up as evidence that the doctrines of the Church aren't true. One way for him to do that is to show where two of our leaders have said something that appears to be in conflict. The fallacy in his doing so is that he has the notion that we believe in the infallibility of prophets. Thus if Brigham Young said something that is not the doctrine of the Church, then the Church can't be true because one of its prophets made an error. Now, Elder, do you see what is happening? Your critic is telling you that we believe in the infallibility of prophets. The truth is, we simply don't believe that. Joseph Smith was the great prophet of this dispensation, yet the Doctrine and Covenants contains a number of revelations in which the Lord scolds him and invites him to repent. In this Church everyone is privileged to make mistakes and repent of them. We take that as an evidence that the Church is true, not that it is false."

By now my young caller had calmed down considerably. "So what you're telling me," he said, "is that if this Adam-God stuff was really a doctrine of the Church, we would be teaching it today."

"You got it," I said. "The word *doctrine* means 'teaching.' We teach our doctrines."

"So can prophets make mistakes on doctrine?" he asked.

"Elder," I said, "I have never known a man whom we sustain as a prophet, seer, and revelator who thought himself infallible. Nor have I met one whose counsel and testimony were not worth listening to."

"Okay," he said and hung up.

The man who presides over the Church holds the keys of the kingdom. "For him to whom these keys are given," modern revelation declares, "there is no difficulty in obtaining a knowledge of facts in relation to the salvation of the children of men, both as well for the dead as for the living" (D&C 128:11). In a revelation given on the day the Church was organized, the Lord defined the relationship that was to exist between its members and its presiding officer. "Wherefore, meaning the church," the Lord said, "thou shalt give heed unto all his words and commandments which he shall give unto you as he receiveth them, walking in all holiness before me; for his word ye shall receive, as if from mine own mouth, in all patience and faith. For by doing these things the gates of hell shall not prevail against you; yea, and the Lord God will disperse the powers of darkness from before you, and cause the heavens to shake for your good, and his name's glory" (D&C 21:4–6).

Second, all true doctrine will have revelation as its source. It will come from the Father in the name of Christ. It must be taught and learned by the Spirit of revelation. True doctrine will always declare God and revelation as its source. It will never be based upon "philosophical speculation," as were the decisions of the ecumenical councils out of which the creeds of historical Christianity have come. To those of the Old World Christ declared, "My doctrine is not mine, but his that sent me" (John 7:16). In another instance he said, "Every plant, which my heavenly Father hath not planted, shall be rooted up" (Matthew

15:13). Teaching the same principle in the New World, he said, "This is my doctrine, and I bear record of it from the Father" (3 Nephi 11:35). Teaching this principle in our dispensation the Lord said:

"Let us reason even as a man reasoneth one with another face to face.

"Now, when a man reasoneth he is understood of man, because he reasoneth as a man; even so will I, the Lord, reason with you that you may understand.

"Wherefore, I the Lord ask you this question—unto what were ye ordained?

"To preach my gospel by the Spirit, even the Comforter which was sent forth to teach the truth.

"And then received ye spirits which ye could not understand, and received them to be of God; and in this are ye justified?

"Behold ye shall answer this question yourselves; nevertheless, I will be merciful unto you; he that is weak among you hereafter shall be made strong.

"Verily I say unto you, he that is ordained of me and sent forth to preach the word of truth by the Comforter, in the Spirit of truth, doth he preach it by the Spirit of truth or some other way?

"And if it be by some other way it is not of God.

"And again, he that receiveth the word of truth, doth he receive it by the Spirit of truth or some other way?

"If it be some other way it is not of God.

"Therefore, why is it that ye cannot understand and know, that he that receiveth the word by the Spirit of truth receiveth it as it is preached by the Spirit of truth?

"Wherefore, he that preacheth and he that receiveth, understand one another, and both are edified and rejoice together" (D&C 50:11–22).

Third, pure doctrine will always come through the channels the Lord has ordained. "This greater priesthood," the Lord said, "administereth the gospel and holdeth the key of the mysteries of the kingdom, even the key of the knowledge of God" (D&C 84:19). Explaining this principle, Joseph Smith said that the "Melchizedek Priesthood . . . is the channel through which all knowledge, doctrine, the plan of salvation and every important matter is revealed from heaven" (*Teachings of the Prophet Joseph Smith*, 166–67).

A commonality among cultist groups is the claim to revelation that makes them independent of the order and channels the Lord has established. The claim carries within itself the seed of its own destruction. As the malcontents claim the right to revelation placing them above the discipline and order of the Church, so their followers will claim the same right to rebel against their organization. Thus we find constant division among their ranks.

The revelations of heaven will always call for unity among the Saints and require that they sustain those called to preside over them.

Fourth, it is not for us to either add to or take from the system of salvation as revealed by the Lord. It is not for man to add to or take from the purity of the revealed word. Having taught the principles of faith, repentance, and baptism, the Savior said: "Verily, verily, I say unto you, that this is my doctrine, and whoso buildeth upon this buildeth upon my rock, and the gates of hell shall not prevail against them. And whoso shall declare more or less than this, and establish it for my doctrine, the same cometh of evil, and is not built upon my rock; but he buildeth upon a sandy foundation, and the gates of hell stand open to receive such when the floods come and the winds beat upon them" (3 Nephi 11:39–40).

This text is marvelously instructive and challenging. On the one hand it directs that we are to neither take from or add to that which has come from the Lord. On the other hand, we are to build upon the foundation he has laid. We must build revelation upon revelation. We cannot say, We have this, or, We have done that, and that is sufficient. "Wo be unto him that saith: We have received, and we need no more!

"And in fine, wo unto all those who tremble, and are angry

because of the truth of God! For behold, he that is built upon the rock receiveth it with gladness; and he that is built upon a sandy foundation trembleth lest he shall fall.

"Wo be unto him that shall say: We have received the word of God, and we need no more of the word of God, for we have enough!

"For behold, thus saith the Lord God: I will give unto the children of men line upon line, precept upon precept, here a little and there a little; and blessed are those who hearken unto my precepts, and lend an ear unto my counsel, for they shall learn wisdom; for unto him that receiveth I will give more; and from them that shall say, We have enough, from them shall be taken away even that which they have" (2 Nephi 28:27–30).

This passage suggests that we may well be missing the point by attempting to answer the question of what doctrine is "official" and what is not. At issue is truth—finding and complying with the principles that bring salvation. The issue is not whether something is official, or once was official, or will yet become official. The issue is whether or not it builds upon the foundation laid by Christ and his apostles. Is it in harmony with all other laws and ordinances of the gospel? Does it sanctify the soul? Does it lead us closer to God? Surely any principle that responds affirmatively to such questions can be numbered among the doctrines of the Latter-day Saints.

Fifth, true doctrine will always edify. The Spirit of the Lord is positive, not negative. It lifts and builds. "That which doth not edify," we are told, "is not of God" (D&C 50:23). Originally the verb "to edify" meant to build sacred edifices, for instance, the temple. With use the word has come to describe the process of improving character or building spirituality. All that is of God edifies—that is, it lifts, builds, and improves; to edify is, conversely, to eschew that which demeans, belittles, or excuses. To edify is to make the body and soul of man a holy tabernacle, a temple to God. Any doctrine that does not lead to this end is not of God. To those who feared that the Book of Mormon might have some kind of negative effect on the stature of the Bible the Lord said, "I do not bring it to destroy that which they have received, but to build it up" (D&C 10:52). Such is the purpose of the restored gospel. Never does a missionary ask prospective converts to surrender any positive habit or practice in joining the Church. Rather they are told to hold tenaciously to such good things and the restored gospel will add to them. "Yea, and I will also bring to light my gospel," the Lord said, "which was ministered unto them, and, behold, they shall not deny that which you have received, but they shall build it up, and shall bring to light the true points of my doctrine, yea, and the only doctrine which is in me" (D&C 10:62). In harmony with this principle the charge given by Christ to the meridian Twelve was to "seek not the things of this world but seek ye first to build up the kingdom of God, and to establish his righteousness" (JST Matthew 6:33).

Sixth, the standard works are the measuring rod for all doctrine. "It makes no difference," stated President Joseph Fielding Smith, "what is written or what anyone has said, if what has been said is in conflict with what the Lord has revealed, we can set it aside. My words, and the teachings of any other member of the Church, high or low, if they do not square with the revelations, we need not accept them. Let us have this matter clear. We have accepted the four standard works as the measuring yardsticks, or balances, by which we measure every man's doctrine.

"You cannot accept the books written by the authorities of the Church as standards in doctrine, only in so far as they accord with the revealed word in the standard works.

"Every man who writes is responsible, not the Church, for what he writes. If Joseph Fielding Smith writes something which is out of harmony with the revelations, then every member of the Church is duty bound to reject it. If he writes that which is in perfect harmony with the revealed word of the Lord, then it should be accepted" (*Doctrines of Salvation*, 3:203–4).

Teaching the same principle, President Harold B. Lee said: "It is not to be thought that every word spoken by the General Authorities is inspired, or that they are moved upon by the Holy Ghost in everything they [speak] and write. Now you keep that in mind. I don't care what his position is, if he writes something or speaks something that goes beyond anything that you can find in the standard church works, unless that one be the prophet, seer, and revelator—please note that one exception—you may immediately say, 'Well, that is his own idea.' And if he says something that contradicts what is found in the standard church works (I think that is why we call them 'standard'—it is the standard measure of all that men teach), you may know by that same token that it is false, regardless of the position of the man who says it" ("Place of the Living Prophet, Seer and Revelator," 14).

Seventh, no true doctrine can stand independent of the testimony that Jesus Christ is the Son of God and that salvation is in and through him and none other. Announcing this truth in our dispensation the Lord said, "Behold, Jesus Christ is the name which is given of the Father, and there is none other name given whereby man can be saved; wherefore, all men must take upon them the name which is given of the Father, for in that name shall they be called at the last day; wherefore, if they know not the name by which they are called, they cannot have place in the kingdom of my Father" (D&C 18:23–25).

All true doctrine testifies of Christ. No doctrine of salvation can stand independent of him.

It is impossible for a person to have the companionship of the Holy Ghost and at the same time deny that Jesus is the Christ (see 1 Corinthians 12:3; Smith, *Teachings of the Prophet Joseph Smith,* 223). Similarly, it is impossible for anyone to enjoy the companionship of the Holy Ghost and at the same time deny that Joseph Smith is the great prophet of the Restoration or that the Book of Mormon is true—or any other saving truth in the restored gospel.

QUESTION

Does the gospel embrace all truth?

ANSWER

No. Innumerable truths have no bearing on that sacred body of truth we call the gospel. It is true, for example, that my father wore a size fifteen shoe, liked to wear bow ties, and had my mother cut his hair. Though such things are true, they have nothing to do with the gospel. None of these things affected his knowledge of the gospel or the testimony he bore. You need neither imitate them nor remember them to be saved.

There is no equality among truths. They are like pebbles on a dirt road. Only rarely will you find one that is of any measurable worth. Gospel truths, the truths that are eternal and have the power of salvation in them, will have God as their author and revelation as their source. They will lift and edify the soul and be accompanied by a spirit of peace. They will also cause the adversary to holler and complain. Any truth that does not offend the prince of darkness, causing him to rant and rave, cannot be of any particular moment.

Similarly, any principle that does not require the Spirit of the Lord to teach can be taught as well by a faithless man as a learned, as well by students of faith as by those who are making no effort to accord their lives with the standards the Lord has set. Such a truth is not a gospel principle and will be of no value in the world to come.

When missionaries go out into the world to declare the "fulness of [the] gospel" (D&C 1:23), we send them out to teach faith, repentance, and baptism. They do not go out to prepare people to receive a college degree. They go out to prepare people to receive a degree of glory that centers on that understanding that comes only from living gospel principles. In so saying, there is no demeaning the value of secular learning. The knowledge of such things has placed many in a position to be of meaningful service both to their community and to the Church. Yet it would miss the mark to suppose that secular knowledge could somehow substitute for purity, faith, and obedience to the laws and ordinances of the gospel.

QUESTION

Does doctrine change?

ANSWER

Doctrine consists of eternal principles, which are the same yesterday, today, and forever. The principles known to us in our second estate were known to us in our first, or premortal, estate. A knowledge of these principles will rise with us in the resurrection to be used by us in the same manner as they are here. Though the principles are eternal, they find application according to time and season.

"To every thing there is a season, and a time to every purpose under the heaven: a time to be born, and a time to die; a time to plant, and a time to pluck up that which is planted; a time to kill, and a time to heal; a time to break down, and a time to build up; a time to weep, and a time to laugh; a time to mourn, and a time to dance; a time to cast away stones, and a time to gather stones together; a time to embrace, and a time to refrain from embracing; a time to get, and a time to lose; a time to keep, and a time to cast away; a time to rend, and a time to sew; a time to keep silence, and a time to speak; a time to love, and a time to hate; a time of war, and a time of peace" (Ecclesiastes 3:1–8).

During one time and season missionaries are commanded to go forth without purse or scrip; in another, to take the same (see Luke 22:35–36). In one instance they are commanded to speak forth boldly; in another, to remain silent (see D&C 75:4; Matthew 17:9). Circumstances may change, but the principle of revelation remains constant. The Prophet taught, "This is the principle on which the government of heaven is conducted—by revelation adapted to the circumstances in which the children of the kingdom are placed" (*Teachings of the Prophet Joseph Smith*, 256). At no period in earth's history could the kingdom of God be adequately governed by the revelations given to another people in another time for other reasons. The constitution of the Church must always be the voice of its living prophet.

QUESTION

Who can declare doctrine?

ANSWER

It has occasionally been argued that only the president of the Church has the authority to expound scripture. This argument appears a little ridiculous when it is remembered that it is the duty of the priests in the Aaronic Priesthood "to preach, teach, expound, exhort, and baptize" and that both teacher and deacon are also called "to warn, expound, exhort, and teach, and invite all to come unto Christ" (D&C 20:46, 59). "To expound" is defined in the dictionary of Joseph Smith's day as "to interpret; as, to expound a text of scripture" (Webster, *American Dictionary*, 78). The argument that only the president of the Church can teach doctrine usually comes from someone who doesn't like the interpretation that someone else has placed on a particular text, so he or she simply argues that whoever said it is without authority to do so. Thus the focus of the discussion is shifted from a consideration of the correctness of a particular statement to a consideration of authority.

It is true, and well understood by Latter-day Saints generally, that all sound doctrine must trace itself to the prophetic voice and that the living head of the Church is the binding voice on all doctrinal matters. That does not mean, however, that every doctrinal insight must originate with him or that no one else's doctrinal understanding can exceed his. It was never intended that only ordained prophets could write inspired books, poetry, plays, hymns, or music for the edification of the members of the Church. Neither was it intended that they give all the patriarchal blessings, deliver all the inspired addresses, teach all the classes, or lead all the choirs. Indeed, it may never be their lot to paint the great paintings, sculpt with inspiration, or design chapels and temples. The kingdom of God is to be built as the tabernacle in the wilderness or the temple in Jerusalem was—by the revelation of God as it manifests itself through a prophet and a nation of artists and craftsmen. All who labor to build the house of the Lord, be it temporal or spiritual, be it ancient or modern, are to do so with the Spirit of revelation. And it goes almost without saying, that as the greatest of temples awaits building, so the best of books, music, art, and all things that testify of our God still await the day of their earthly creation.

Question

When we teach, is it ever proper to go beyond the literal rendering of the scripture itself?

Answer

Even scripture is not scripture unless we bring the Spirit of inspiration and revelation to it. Illustrating this principle, Elder Bruce R. McConkie said: "Those who preach by the power of the Holy Ghost use the scriptures as their basic source of knowledge and doctrine. They begin with what the Lord has before revealed to other inspired men. But it is the practice of the Lord to give added knowledge to those upon whose hearts the true meanings and intents of the scriptures have been impressed. Many great doctrinal revelations come to those who preach from the scriptures. When they are in tune with the Infinite, the Lord lets them know, first, the full and complete meaning of the scriptures they are expounding, and then he ofttimes expands their views so that new truths flood in upon them, and they learn added things that those who do not follow such a course can never know. Hence, as to 'preaching the word,' the Lord commands his servants to go forth 'saying none other things than that which the prophets and apostles have written, and that which is taught them by the Comforter through the prayer of faith.' (D&C 52:9.) In a living, growing, divine church, new truths will come from time to time and old truths will be applied with new vigor to new situations, all under the guidance of the Holy Spirit of God" (*Promised Messiah*, 515–16).

QUESTION

Are all the answers we need found in the scriptures?

ANSWER

No. This is the party line of apostate religion, and it is called the doctrine of sufficiency. The claim is that the Bible contains all that is or ever can be necessary for the benefit of man. In making such a claim, they are sealing the heavens, silencing God, doing away with the need for living prophets, and denying the power of the Holy Ghost. For a Latter-day Saint to say the same thing of the standard works is to agree in principle with this basic dogma of the Apostasy. Nephi said of such a notion, "For unto him that receiveth I will give more; and from them that shall say, We have enough, from them shall be taken away even that which they have" (2 Nephi 28:30).

QUESTION

How should doctrinal issues be settled?

227

ANSWER

Perhaps an illustration will help. I received a call from a woman asking about a doctrine we had studied in a class she had taken a few years before. She told me that the question had come up in a Gospel Doctrine class and she had mentioned what she had learned in class only to be severely rebuked by some of the class members. Then others got involved, and people divided themselves into two camps. At that point the bishop intervened and said that he would teach the lesson the next week and settle the issue and that after he had taught there were to be no questions. I don't know what happened the following week and am probably happier not knowing.

The problem here is at least twofold. First, it is unfortunate that Latter-day Saints would divide themselves in a spirit of sharpness in a discussion over doctrine. That would have to be offensive to the Spirit of truth. It is also unfortunate that the bishop chose to settle the issue with what might be called a priesthood power play. Not the least of the difficulties here is that such are subject to reversal every time a new bishop is called. Would it not have been more appropriate for a charge to be given to each member of the class to go home and prayerfully search the scriptures and for the class to come together again the next week in a spirit of searching rather than in a spirit of defending? The Lord has frequently enjoined us to search the scriptures; he has never directed that we debate them.

I am sure no one would question that the final word on all doctrinal matters rests with the president of the Church. Certainly the united voice of the First Presidency and/or the Quorum of the Twelve carries the same authority. Independent of decisions made by such authority, the standard works constitute the measuring rod. Bishops and stake presidents and the disciplinary councils over which they have the authority to preside are responsible to handle matters of apostasy, which could include the persistent teaching of false doctrine. There is always a right of appeal that attends their decisions, so, if necessary, any disagreement could be reviewed by the highest authorities in the Church.

AT ISSUE

The whole system of salvation centers in our obtaining the "mind of Christ," as Paul said (1 Corinthians 2:16). It is the process by which we come to think as God thinks, to believe as he believes, and therefore to act as he would act. It embraces, Paul explained, our "rightly dividing the word of truth" (2 Timothy 2:15). The original sense of this text was to "cut a straight path," or to "hold to a straight course." It was a charge to teach the truths of salvation without adding to or taking from them (see 3 Nephi 11:39–40). It also embraced the idea of dividing to every man according to his need (see D&C 84:85). A proper understanding of the text gives us a clearer view of the ministry of John the Baptist, who was charged to "make straight in the desert a highway for our God" (Isaiah 40:3). That is, his office was to teach the doctrine that would prepare the hearts and minds of men to accept Christ and his teachings. All good doctrine has this as its end. No good doctrine "rightly divided" would ever do otherwise. Good doctrine "cuts a straight path" and demands that we "hold to a straight course." Believing in good doctrine always lifts us to a higher level of commitment while at the same time placing us in a position to see and understand all other doctrines more clearly.

Most doctrinal errors are rooted in a desire to accommodate either the standards of the world or its philosophies and theories. In a sobering, prophetic description of our day, Nephi said, "They have all gone astray save it be a few, who are the humble followers of Christ; nevertheless, they are led, that in many instances they do err because they are taught by the precepts of men" (2 Nephi 28:14). The Lord warned Joseph Smith that the prince of darkness would come to "[take] away light and truth, through disobedience," doing so under the cloak of the "tradition of their fathers" (D&C 93:39). In the process of discerning what constitutes sound doctrine, among the basic questions that ought to be asked is, Where does this lead? Does it lead us to favor with God or man? Robert J. Matthews properly observes that "in the process of apostasy, the most spiritual doctrines are cast aside first. Ethical teachings remain even in apostasy, but the most profound doctrinal precepts are discarded as narrow, theoretical, opinionated, discriminatory, uninspired, and socially unacceptable" (unpublished lecture).

The only true danger facing Mormonism is that which comes from within. It comes from those who would seek to popularize Mormonism so that we might be like, and thus acceptable to, the world. Such people should remember, observed President Joseph F. Smith, "that the theories of the worldly-wise cannot with safety be engrafted into the principles of the gospel. We have received a distinct dispensation of the gospel." Ours is a revealed faith, a new dispensation, which by its very definition demands that we stand independent of the world. "We cannot," President Smith observed, "consent to be guided by inspiration from the outside, but are in duty bound to follow in the way revealed by God. To be directed by the postulates of the world, and by leaders of men, will be just as fatal to the Latter-day Saints, as it was for the Former-day Saints" ("Principle, Not Popularity," 731).

Of necessity there will always be things about our faith that will be offensive to the world. "Do you suppose that this people will ever see the day that they will rest in perfect security, in hopes of becoming like another people, nation, state, kingdom, or society?" Brigham Young asked. *"They never will,"* he declared. "Christ and Satan never can be friends. Light and darkness will always remain opposites" (in *Journal of Discourses*, 1:188).

SOURCES

Charlesworth, James H. *Jesus within Judaism*. New York: Doubleday, 1988.

Clark, James R., comp. *Messages of the First Presidency of The Church of Jesus Christ of Latter-day Saints*. 6 vols. Salt Lake City: Bookcraft, 1965–75.

Coakely, Sarah, and David Palin, eds. *The Making and Remaking of Christian Doctrine*. Oxford: Clarendon Press, 1993.

Cross, F. L., ed. *Oxford Dictionary of the Christian Church*. London: Oxford University Press, 1958.

Dew, Sheri L. *Ezra Taft Benson: A Biography*. Salt Lake City: Deseret Book, 1987.

Evening and the Morning Star, The. 1 (July 1832): [1–3].

Ehat, Andrew, and Lyndon W. Cook. *Words of Joseph Smith*. Orem, Utah: Grandin Book, 1991.

First Presidency [Joseph F. Smith, John R. Winder, and Anthon H. Lund]. "Origin of Man," *Improvement Era* 13 (November 1909): 75–81.

Hinckley, Bryant S. *Sermons and Missionary Services of Melvin Joseph Ballard*. Salt Lake City: Deseret Book, 1949.

Hymns of The Church of Jesus Christ of Latter-day Saints. Salt Lake City: The Church of Jesus Christ of Latter-day Saints, 1985.

Ivins, Anthony W. In Conference Report, October 1925, 19–28.

Jessee, Dean C. "Joseph Smith's 19 July 1840 Discourse," *BYU Studies* 19 [spring 1979]: 390–94.

Journal of Discourses. 26 vols. London: Latter-day Saints' Book Depot, 1854–86.

Kimball, Spencer W. "Be Ye Therefore Perfect." Address delivered at University of Utah Institute of Religion, Salt Lake City, Utah, 10 January 1975. Typescript.

Kubo, Sakae, and Walter F. Specht. *So Many Versions?* Grand Rapids, Mich.: Zondervan, 1975.

Lee, Harold B. In Conference Report, April 1973, 4–10.

―――. "The Place of the Living Prophet, Seer, and Revelator." Address delivered to seminary and institute of religion faculty, Brigham Young University, Provo, Utah, 8 July 1964. Typescript.

Matthews, Robert J. Unpublished lecture delivered to religion faculty, Brigham Young University, Provo, Utah, 19 February 1993.

Maxwell, Neal A. *Deposition of a Disciple*. Salt Lake City: Deseret Book, 1976.

McConkie, Bruce R. *A New Witness for the Articles of Faith*. Salt Lake City: Deseret Book, 1985.

―――. *Mormon Doctrine*, 2d ed. Salt Lake City: Bookcraft, 1966.

―――. In Conference Report, April 1978, 15–18.

―――. "The Foolishness of Teaching." Address delivered to Church Educational System personnel, Salt Lake City, 1981.

―――. Untitled address to leadership training meeting, Brigham Young University, Provo, Utah, 2 October 1981.

New English Bible. Oxford: Oxford University Press, 1970.

Oaks, Dallin H. In Conference Report, April 1992, 47–52.

Packer, Boyd K. "The Law and the Light." In *The Book of Mormon, Jacob through Words of Mormon: To Learn with Joy* [papers from the Fourth Annual Book of Mormon Symposium, 1988]. Edited by Monte S. Nyman and Charles D. Tate Jr. (Provo, Utah: Brigham Young University Religious Studies Center, 1988), 1–31.

———. Address at the funeral of Bruce R. McConkie, Salt Lake City, 23 April 1985. LDS Church Historical Library.

Romney, Marion G. In Conference Report, April 1976, 117–21.

———. "A Glorious Promise." *Ensign*, January 1981, 2–3.

———. "The Price of Peace." *Ensign*, October 1983, 2–7.

Smith, Joseph. *Lectures on Faith*. Compiled by N. B. Lundwall. Salt Lake City: N. B. Lundwall, n.d.

———. *History of The Church of Jesus Christ of Latter-day Saints*. Edited by B. H. Roberts. 2d ed. rev. Salt Lake City: The Church of Jesus Christ of Latter-day Saints, 1932–51.

———. *Teachings of the Prophet Joseph Smith*. Sel. Joseph Fielding Smith. Salt Lake City: Deseret Book, 1938.

———. "A Vision." *Times and Seasons* 4 (1 February 1843): 82–85.

Smith, Joseph F. "Principle, Not Popularity." *Improvement Era* 9 [July 1906]: 731–33.

Smith, Joseph Fielding. *Doctrines of Salvation*. Compiled by Bruce R. McConkie. 3 vols. Salt Lake City: Bookcraft, 1954–56.

———. *The Way to Perfection*. Salt Lake City: Deseret Book, 1975.

———. In Conference Report, October 1966, 83–84.

Webster, Noah. *American Dictionary of the English Language*. New York: S. Converse, 1828. Reprint, San Francisco: Foundation for American Christian Education, 1980.

Whitney, Orson F. In Conference Report, April 1929, 109–15.

INDEX